Life in a Nutshell

Life in a Nutshell
By One of Its Biggest Nuts

Hal Mortier
Cover Art by Amanda Ellis

Columbus, Ohio

The views and opinions expressed in this book are solely those of the author and do not reflect the views or opinions of Gatekeeper Press. Gatekeeper Press is not to be held responsible for and expressly disclaims responsibility of the content herein.

Life in a Nutshell: By One of Its Biggest Nuts

Published by Gatekeeper Press
2167 Stringtown Rd, Suite 109
Columbus, OH 43123-2989
www.GatekeeperPress.com

Copyright © 2020 by Hal Mortier

All rights reserved. Neither this book, nor any parts within it may be sold or reproduced in any form or by any electronic or mechanical means, including information storage and retrieval systems without permission in writing from the author. The only exception is by a reviewer, who may quote short excerpts in a review.

The editorial work for this book is entirely the product of the author. Gatekeeper Press did not participate in and is not responsible for any aspect of this element.

Library of Congress Control Number: t/k

ISBN (paperback): 9781662902277

Contents

Introduction — vii

Chapter 1 Just A Bit About Me — 1
Forgiveness

Chapter 2 My Heroes Have Always Been Hotshots — 13
Teamwork

Chapter 3 If The Grass Seems Greener — 25
Contentment

Chapter 4 Never Stop Growing — 39
Perseverance

Chapter 5 Mefirstness — 49
Compassion

Chapter 6 Ain't It The Truth — 59
Honesty

Chapter 7 We Are Family — 67
Commitment

Chapter 8 Let Freedom Ring — 75
Gratitude

Chapter 9 Counting My Steps — 83
Health

Chapter 10 Go Slow To Go Fast — 93
Patience

Chapter 11 With God Good, Without God Bad — 101
Faith

Chapter 12 Thank You & Good-Bye — 107

Introduction

I decided that this introduction is a make or break deal from the start for my book writing adventure. If I cannot nail the intro it seems senseless to go forward with a book. You will help me decide as I encourage you strongly to toss the book if it doesn't fully engage you and proceed vigorously if it does… and if you are related to me in any way please read this book regardless. Why even consider writing a book? It is a lot of work, extremely poor odds of success, and potentially a big waste of time. Well I have never shied away from hard work, always been a pretty poor gambler, and at this stage of my life I seem to have lots of time!

    As I begin to look at the age of sixty in my rear-view mirror and far too quickly approach the big seven zero, I have noticed a number of things. I pee a lot more than I used to and more to the point I seem to suddenly be very contemplative. I don't know if they have a pill for it and if they do, I should probably take it. I likely wouldn't notice mixed in with the plethora of other pills that are now such an intimate part of my daily life. To my good fortune I try to stay in reasonably good shape for an "old guy" and stay sharp in the mind as much as possible. But something about this aging keeps me day in and day out pondering the good, the bad, and even the mundane of my life throughout the years. Worst yet, I have a compelling desire to share it with others. So sorry in advance for that. Most of my life I didn't think beyond the moment and now I can't escape this incessant contemplation.

I recently read a humorous book written by a good friend of mine about his time as a California State Park Ranger. He too is on the back side of sixty. It was incredibly funny and shared telling adventures of his time working in the state parks. He later wrote a more serious much longer book about some of the great individuals he worked with over the years and it was an excellent read and highly informative. And yet another friend wrote and published a couple of fictional novels that I read and enjoyed. Yes, in his sixties as well. And you guessed it, more contemplation for me. For starters if my friends Dave and Matt can do it, so can I? Do the events, the lessons, the goods, the bad, the excitement, and the ordinary of my life warrant documentation? And more importantly is it worthy of sharing with others? Do I have the skills and abilities to make it happen? Who knows? Why don't we see!

I have some innate gifts yes, but frankly I had to learn what I now know about life the hard way. As they say, from the school of hard knocks! When you stray off course, it's that feeling in your gut and thought in your head that help bring you back in line. In my case it was too often more than a stray and more like a plummet. It took a lot of hard knocks to get me to where I am today. I had basically as ordinary life as anyone could possibly have. Still within it were isolated difficulties, life lessons, and experiences that taught me so many good things and yes even some worthy of sharing. And it should be noted that I have had my share of blessings as well. Over the last several years I have written short articles about some of these and kept notes on many others over time.

After my other friend published his book I thought over and over do I have something valuable to share? Maybe so, maybe not, but might be fun to try! I suspect something else we are compelled to do in our sixties (beside peeing more and taking copious amounts of pills) is write a book or at least attempt to do so.

So back to contemplation. What insights do I possess that could be of any value to another person? What expertise do I have to share that could be a benefit to others? It would need to be both edifying and somewhat entertaining? And of course, there is the credibility issue to consider as well. What makes me worthy of passing along unsolicited words of wisdom to readers who didn't really ask for it in the first place? A lot of questions needing great thought from a not so deep-thinking source, me! Well first of all in the course of my previously stated somewhat ordinary life, "stuff" did happen. "Stuff" is a very technical term for the vicissitudes and permutations of my life. Don't worry I found the last two words in my Thesaurus to see if you were awake and promise not to do so again. But basically, within the composite of my time here on Earth some real "stuff" has happened. Can I be entertaining? I do love humor, be it somewhat silly or lame humor according to my wife, kids and grandkids. If I can flavor my thoughts with said humor and articulate it in an amusing and engaging way, it just might work. Do I have the credibility? I am in fact more than highly qualified to speak to issues as one of life's *"Biggest Nuts"*. And lastly, is what I have to share remotely interesting to others? I guess we will have to see how that all turns out.

So how did I arrive at the architecture of this book? Well for starters my thoughts and ideas had no compelling plot with a single story leading up to it. Fortunate for me as I would not know how or have the skill to write a book like that anyway. My life had no real drama or mystery that I might weave into a master novel you couldn't put down, so that was out. Autobiography would be a total bust no doubt. Fiction was a NO as I have enough on my plate dealing with real life. So how could I best produce something of value that others would enjoy and hopefully find interesting? *Life in a Nutshell, by One of Its Biggest Nuts* is a collection of short stories of my 68+ years inclusive of both my failings and of my growth. Hopefully, that in some way might be of interest to you…and maybe just maybe benefit you a little bit at that same time. By design each chapter can be read as a stand-alone story with a unique message relating to a core character attribute. I have identified or related to almost a dozen of these key attributes…Forgiveness, Teamwork, Contentment, Perseverance, Compassion, Honesty, Commitment, Gratitude, Health, Patience, and Faith. The message for each was not necessarily brilliantly discovered by me, but more discoveries I had within my life that gave me some perspective on the subject. Some are true accounts of actual occurrences while a few are just stories to illustrate my point. They are not particularly chronological or in any order. Read the ones that pique your interest in any order you please. And if you happen to read them all, may they be a blessing to you, as your enjoyment of them would certainly be a blessing to me. Each chapter is prefaced with an especially lame joke or one-liner. Let's have some fun with that and please cut me some slack as I am getting really old and so is my humor. See if you can find the relationship to the chapter as you read it…and if you do please share that with me as there was really no intent to do so. Basically, they are included only to annoy my wife, my children, and my grandchildren, but they will have to read the book for this to happen! I can probably shame them into doing so but hope you can see some value in giving this a shot!

***

At the completion of each chapter (and this Introduction as well) I have shared how each character attribute is associated with that story and how it has affected my life. For the Introduction I have selected "courage". One definition of courage I found was simple and succinct. "The ability to do something that frightens one". I like it! I also can't help but think of the Cowardly Lion in the Wizard of Oz and his battle with courage. He wanted courage so bad in his life he was willing to travel with a motley group of people, to an unknown land, in the craziest of conditions, and deal with an eccentric crazy old wizard. Though he didn't always reflect it, courage was that important to him. For me courage has been a lifelong desire of mine in which many times throughout I certainly lacked to a large degree. Why is courage my attribute for the Introduction? Because believe me it took a ton of courage to attempt this feat, this book writing adventure. Whether or not it is a success doesn't matter…I am thankful I had the courage to give it a try!

Just A Bit About Me
Forgiveness

CHAPTER 1

"A clear conscience is usually a sign of a bad memory"

I didn't want to go down that path of "I was really young when I was born" and bore you with all the intimate details of my at times pretty boring and mundane life. So, I will do my best not to. Let's start on a fun note or at least I traditionally have had some fun with it. My name, Hal. I am told it was selected because my paternal grandfather's middle name was Henry and my Uncle on my mother's side was Harold. Not exactly sure how that all spins out, but I ended up with Hal. I often thought three letters was all my folks thought I could handle, not being the brightest lamp in the room. I have since taken it upon myself to blend my name into parts of the English language and at least get a cursory laugh from my grandkids and usually a heavy sigh from my wife Dolores. I will proudly proclaim loudly to all, "Hal-alujah" and remind them it is not "Jackson-alujah" or "Dolores-alujah" but "Hal-alujah. Or I will ask my grandson Jackson as we head up the mountain to ski, "what "haltitude" are we at? And if he replies, "I don't know Papa, 6,000' maybe 7,000'. " I then advise him to check his "haltimeter" and he would know what the exact "haltitude' is. I promised you lame and lame you get.

Life in a Nutshell

As I share and bare some facts about my family, I want to be clear that I had loving parents and a pretty quality life overall. It just included a lot of "stuff" (previously defined in the introduction), some good and some not so good. I believe the composite of both good and bad is what gives me the opportunity to speak as one of life's biggest nuts. My life offered an array of occasions for my developmental growth. My family resembled many post World War II families in both size and situation. Dad returned with issues any young man would have post war. Our family eventually grew to be me and four siblings until much later in life we learned of a fifth sibling. Mom had a child out of wedlock who had been given up for adoption. Mom and Dad loved each other but bouts of drinking often led to arguing and arguing into chaos. Again, we were always cared for and loved, but home could be volatile more often than not. Mom was PTA president and Dad our Little League coach, so my parents were very present in our life. We had some examples of unconditional love and sadly many examples of extremely "conditional" love as well. Mom and Dad were borderline "divorced" for most of my youth but actually survived their marriage until mom's death. Dad and his father struggled over and over due to unresolvable issues, unresolvable at least in their minds. The two of them had completely severed their relationship by the time Grandpa passed. Dad and one of my brothers did the same and they were not speaking at all at the time of dad's death. And that brother now sadly, is on the outs with much of the family. No judgment here as certainly all parties bear some the burden of responsibility for the dissolution of these relationships, but we lacked good examples of unconditional love as that never-ending bond that ties loved ones together forever.

So, on one hand we had stability. We had parental presence and love. We had engagement and participation in our life. We had clothes on our back, food on our table, and a home to sleep in always. We went camping and fishing and had many joyous occasions. On the other hand, we had drinking, arguing, fighting, and broken or tattered relationships that lacked strength to endure. And probably the most amazing fact is I think our family was pretty normal for that post war era.

Back more specifically to me because it really is all about me isn't it? Just kidding...or am I? I was a "normal" youth if there is such a thing. I had my strengths and I had my weaknesses and shortcomings. In sixth grade I was school class president! In sixth grade I peed the bed at 6th Grade Camp. I played sports, some competitively and generally got very good grades all throughout school. I was a leader in elementary school, Junior High, and High School...and I also was short, left-handed, buck teeth, and had a butch haircut. I attended church, well actually Sunday School regularly. Mom took us and dad did not attend. Overall, I was at the top of my game exceedingly early on except maybe for my few "short" comings, no pun intended.

I developed a fairly good work ethic at a fairly young age. With the help of a neighbor (who later became an in-law) who managed a restaurant, I was hired at the age of 13. I progressed rapidly from dishwasher to bus boy, to salad maker, to broiler cook and was skilled in all-around restaurant operations. I was paid well for my age, worked a lot of hours, and maintained my grades and schoolwork during this time. Looking back, I may have grown up a bit too fast and was perhaps not mentally prepared to handle this. I started liking beer and other alcohol at an increasing level and frequency. I dabbled in Marijuana too, but neither issue to the point of a real problem during high school. The waitresses generally in their twenties and thirties loved teasing and flirting with the young high schooler and they probably helped escalate my growth in other areas of life too!

A great memory I will always have was our family vacations to the Kern River. I especially enjoyed the fishing and swimming in the river and nearby lake. Dad and Mom, if they managed to not fight, were at their best and it was often a very quality family experience. We met many friends (including a girlfriend or two) as we returned annually for many years. In the course of these vacations I became enthralled with the Forest Rangers who took care of the forest, campground facilities, and fought the wildfires that occurred periodically throughout the forest. I would pester the Rangers, who stopped by regularly to visit my sister and her girlfriends, about doing what they do some day. Both the job and visiting with pretty girls! They would humor me as long as it kept the girls engaged. They would even volunteer to come back and share more after work hours, providing of course the girls were there. Needless to say, they captured the adventurous side of me, and I wanted to grow up to be a Forest Ranger.

In my sophomore year in High School my best friend John's brother got a job as a "hotshot", a seasonal firefighter with the US Forest Service. As far as I was concerned, he was a Forest Ranger but knew little more than that. He was on a crew, the El Cariso Hotshots, that had lost most of their crew in a tragic burnover a couple of years prior. Although obviously scary to some degree, both his brother and I were enamored greatly by this and wore him down with questions at any given opportunity about how we could join up. Through John's brother Bob another good friend joined the hotshot crew the summer after our junior year. John and I used that same connection to get hired starting immediately upon our graduation from high school the following year. More on hotshots to follow in a later chapter.

My career in the Forest Service began July of 1970 on the El Cariso hotshots. Although initially work was seasonal, and I would just return to my restaurant job outside of fire season. I became full-time with the Forest Service about the same time I got married and shortly thereafter had our first child, my daughter Wendy. I experienced relative success in the Forest Service from the beginning. I was a hotshot, an Engineer on a fire engine, a Fire Prevention Technician, Engine Captain, Hotshot Superintendent, and then Battalion Chief in the first nine years of my career. I now had three adorable kids (Wendy, Mark, & Joel), owned a home, had a great job, and a particularly good life or so it seemed!

On-duty, Forest Service was all business and other than sneaking a beer or two into a fire camp during a fire we were pretty well behaved and under control. Off-duty, that was another story. Alcohol consumption was just an everyday part of life and of course on an ever-increasing basis. I had a family history of alcohol abuse but never even gave it a second thought. I was young, aggressive, mildly successful and felt I could handle anything. I am wishing now that it was not the case. The parties, the drinking, and the carousing became too big a part of life and only my on-duty work time had any restraint to it. Thinking I could do most anything and along with two of my Battalion Chief peers, I opted to leave the Forest Service and go into a business partnership with them late in 1979. Too Tall Tree Service was established, and we were going to conquer the world! We had the skill, probably had the smarts, had the work ethic, but lacked the self-control...speaking for myself anyway. More to follow about Too Tall Tree Service in another chapter.

The lack of self-control, the drinking, the partying, the complete demise of good life priorities resulted in divorce. I had really let my family down and sadly did not completely realize it at the time. Without the minimal control the Forest Service had provided within my life I spiraled down a fairly rapid descent. It was now more than just alcohol; it was other drugs too. It was now all day long and now every day. My three children remained important to me and I loved them dearly. It was probably the only life responsibility I halfway fulfilled and admittedly not nearly as well as I should have. I entered a relationship with a lady who partied and participated equally with me to neither of our good fortune. We fought a lot and borderline broke up on a routine basis until she became pregnant with my fourth child, Lacey. For Lacey, we did our best to make things work, but did nothing about the alcohol and drug abuse. We got married in hopes it would make things better at least for our daughter. This life continued and I don't have to describe it to you as it mirrored anyone who slips to this depth of self-destruction...whether accidently or on purpose.

So, one night in the midst of one of our more volatile skirmishes, and high on drugs and alcohol, I had a "come to Jesus" experience. True story, I didn't recognize it as such until much later but believe me. We were living in a camper shell located on property we had been evicted from. Our daughter Lacey was trying to sleep in the camper overhead in spite of our screaming and yelling horridly at each other. Mid-cursing and such Lacey awoke and began crying. I heard her and looked at her and just said out loud spontaneously, "this is not where I am supposed to be!" Basically, I repeated to the effect that I was not supposed to end up like this and put my child in the situation she was in. I said to my wife, "I am done. I am not going to do this anymore!" She, highly confused thought I was speaking specifically about our argument, but I meant everything. The drugs, the alcohol, the fighting, the living on property in which we were not allowed…everything. I didn't know why; I just knew I was done.

I have not taken a sip of alcohol or an illegal or unprescribed drug since that night. The next day I explained to my wife that I have decided to stop completely, and she could as well if she desired. I had no expectation that she would automatically have to follow my lead. To her credit she said she wanted to give it a try also. Decisions were made quickly, but to this day I feel guided by a much higher power than me. It just happened to be Mother's Day and I had certainly burnt some bridges with my family. Many were tired of my way of life and my excuses. I called the bulk of my family together and told them of my epiphany. I did not expect them to swallow my story hook, line, and sinker so instead just asked for their willingness to let me earn back their respect. They all agreed to give it a shot and for that I remain grateful to this day.

I had lifetime re-instatement rights with the Forest Service and immediately felt it would be a positive move to return to that job to have more structure in my life. Ironically when meeting to re-establish myself back into the USFS my wife was offered a job as well. So very quickly employment for us both was not an issue and quickly resolved. I also suggested that we find a church to surround us with more positive influences to help us through this. Again, to her credit she agreed. We did so almost immediately, and it did exactly that.

As we re-engaged in a more responsible life it seemed to go better for me than my wife. I was very committed for reasons I couldn't even explain. She found herself leaning towards much of the old life. Basically, we had agreed that if that were the case, we would go our separate ways. We ended our relationship in divorce and at least initially our daughter remained with me. Her mother moved away for a time to the state of Washington. In due time she returned to our daughter's life and shared some of the parental responsibility of raising her.

So, two divorces and 4 beautiful children later I am sitting with two strikes on me and thinking I should just take a pitch or two; hopefully you get the pitiful baseball analogy. You know the old three strikes and you're out thing. I engaged full throttle into church, as my history kind of indicates that I do with most things. But in this case it was healthy, wholesome, and for a lack of a better term it kept me out of the bars, so to speak. I was exercising, excelling at work, and highly active in my church. Then it happened! A very pretty and sweet lady I spoke to occasionally at Bible Study joined us for a home build in Mexico, in which I was the lead builder. I was too busy to spend much time with her, so she followed my sister around asking her questions and such about me. Post build and after hearing reports from my sister I engaged her in conversation after the next Bible Study. She had a tree she needed an estimate on and I happened to be an experienced tree expert. Well to cut (no pun intended) to the chase…the tree led to dinner, dinner led to falling in love, and falling in love led to marriage number three. But instead of three strikes you're out it was absolutely *the third time is a charm!* Dolores has two sons and together we have 4 boys (Mark, Joel, Jesse, & Wes) and 2 girls (Wendy & Lacey). Our marriage has not been perfect by any means but as close to perfect as possible on this Earth and we are now approaching our 25th wedding anniversary. She is the love of my life and my writing editor always, whether it is just an e-mail or a book!

I continued and finished up a successful career with the Forest Service with many treasured moments. I was in the role of Deputy Chief at the time of my retirement. Just prior I was a Division Chief in my day job and a National Type 1 Incident Commander for large scale incident response. I managed a team of about 50 fire experts who when called out would provide the oversight for some of the largest fire events in the country…and many all-risk events such as hurricanes, earthquake, and even the helped manage the Columbia shuttle recovery. I had assignments in 29 different states and even one on St. Croix in the Virgin Islands. I apologize if this sounds boastful in any way, but instead shared to emphasize the unlimited possibilities for anyone who is able to beat drugs and alcohol. Perhaps my best personal achievement is that my daughter Wendy is a Division Chief on the Stanislaus National Forest. My son Joel a Captain on the Cleveland National Forest. And my stepson Jesse spent over 5 years in the Forest Service as a firefighter. All three spent time on hotshot crews, a fact I am extremely proud of. It is a special honor when your child, in my case children, follow in your footsteps when and if the footsteps lead to a good place!

I left the Forest Service just short of mandatory retirement age when offered a job by the local public utility company. They were having issues with wildfires both with their equipment being related to fire cause as well as damage to their facilities as a result of wildfires. They hired me to be their fire expert or officially Fire Coordinator. This was a brand-new position and I had the luxury of designing what exactly this would be. It was amazing how quickly the job responsibilities grew. A major wildfire impacted the utility company greatly and fire coordination and subject matter expertise increase exponentially. Soon I had sub-staff and became Fire Program Manager with 6 additional retired Fire Chiefs reporting to me. We served as liaison on every fire where the utility was involved. We worked on fire prevention issues and concerns. We served as subject matter experts in legal inquiries and court cases. In a short time, we kept a very talented crew of fire experts more than busy with an ever-increasing workload. I worked for the utility for 13 years after my 30+ years with the Forest Service.

I now enjoy retirement with my beautiful wife. We travel, we serve our Lord, and we have a lot of fun with family, especially our 8 grandchildren and possibly more before all is said and done. I consult for another major utility company and a private Fire Services Company and work only when I want to…and/or when my wife says we need more vacation money!

The ups and downs of my life have both served as blessings to me. I did not particularly enjoy the bad times nor am I proud of some of the things I have done. But without them, I wouldn't be who I am today and who I am today isn't all that bad. I am proud of my resilience. I am thankful for those who stood by me. I thank the Lord for loving me in spite of me. Life is good!

***

My character attribute for Chapter 1 is "Forgiveness". I struggled with choosing this over "Unconditional Love" as both have been so important to my life story shared above. I went with Forgiveness as I truly feel it can be the cement that can nurture and protect all of our relationships when given freely. We all have our moments and can at times use a dose of forgiveness. I have found the lack of forgiveness causes and retains excessive pain, resulting in that pain lingering and eroding our love for each other much too long. And when forgiveness is given freely, it instead heals wounds very quickly and can strengthen relationships beyond our wildest imagination. The effects of forgiveness and the lack of forgiveness is so apparent in my life experience. As I watched father and son at multiple levels of our family hierarchy bitterly end their relationships over misunderstandings and foolish pride. Foolish pride wrongly instilled in so many of us throughout generations. By the same token I watched where "forgiveness" has been such a strength. I thank my first wife Celia for forgiveness that allowed us to continue together to raise our children and for her, me, and even my wife Dolores to remain friends to this day! Similarly, with wife number two.

An interesting fact I have learned over the years about forgiveness is this. When we struggle to forgive we are the one who suffers most. In our efforts to punish another for their wrongdoings we hold anger within that only erodes our happiness. Many times, the violating party is completely unaware of what is going on and innocently moving on with their life while we wallow in our own self-induced misery.

My Heroes Have Always Been Hotshots

CHAPTER 2

Teamwork

"I once went to watch a fight and a Hockey game broke out!"

Well long-ago Willie Nelson made it perfectly clear his heroes had always been Cowboys. He shared this in a beautiful ballad, beautiful assuming of course you enjoy Willie's singing like I do. For your sake I will not attempt to sing mine in a ballad but can assure you *My Heroes Have Always Been Hotshots*. As mentioned earlier in this book I have always been enthralled with Wildland Firefighting. Even my career project in Jr. High was about becoming a Forest Ranger and the firefighting portion being the main attraction to that career. And then, within the firefighting arena Hotshots even more so. They are the elite. They are the Green Berets, Navy Seals, or Army Rangers of the wildland firefighting community. They get the toughest assignments, on the hottest part of the fire, in the steepest terrain, for the longest period of time. Personal bias, yes some! But it is still very accurate I assure you! So, what exactly is a hotshot? A hotshot crew goes where other firefighting resources cannot. Wildfires require a very diverse set of firefighting equipment and personnel, as opposed to structure fires that primarily just use water and fire trucks. Fire Engines for the wildland need to be somewhat compact, able to work in rugged terrain. They are required to access areas that the much larger structure fire engines could not. Wildfires move rapidly and often into areas that are inaccessible to most ground resources. So, aircraft is used and plays a big role in slowing the spread of an advancing wildfire. It also helps by removing some of the heat so firefighters can get closer to the fire's edge and take suppression action. Aircraft and Fire Engines can cool the fire some, but a wildfire is not considered contained or controlled until an appropriate area void of fuel (grass, brush, timber, etc.) is established between the fire's edge and the existing unburned vegetation. This is known as a fireline. Firelines are constructed by hand crews and bulldozers. Hand crews come in all shapes and sizes with an assortment of training and capabilities. Inmate crews (made of low risk incarcerated prisoners) are very capable but have some limits regarding their use. A Type 2 Crew is a designation for fire crews that are more local in nature and too have limits in their use. These can be local forest crews or even trained farm workers with some basic training and proper supervision, but again come with limits in their use. So, hotshots are considered Type 1 in the hand crew world, the top of the line wildland firefighters. They have the most rigorous and extensive training. Therefore, they are used in the most rugged terrain and frequently cut fireline directly against the fire's edge.

Aircraft, both Air Tankers and Helicopters, work in conjunction with hotshots as their work progresses to increase their effectiveness and safety.

My experience with the Hotshots began my very first year in the Forest Service. I had the good fortune of being on the El Cariso Hotshots, one of only three "Interregional" Hotshot Crews in the nation at that time. That designation meant we could go anywhere there was a major fire, whereas other crews had to remain more local usually within the state they reside. This has since changed where basically all hotshot crews are Interregional as the need for them has continued to increase over time. I was a firefighter on El Cariso each of my first two fire seasons in the Forest Service, before leaving to diversify my skills within the Fire Service. I later returned as Hotshot Superintendent, again with El Cariso, and served as the leader for this distinguished crew. It was perhaps the greatest honor of my Forest Service career even though I advanced through the years to a much higher level. All wildland firefighters should be required to serve on a hotshot crew as the experience is immeasurable and you learn a lot about Fire Behavior (the science behind growth and spread of wildfire) very quickly.

So, one day several years ago my college-age daughter Wendy called to share the woes of her life, with dad. She was going to school full-time and was struggling to make ends meet financially and keep up with her schoolwork. She asks me about seasonal firefighting. "Don't hotshots make a lot of money during fire season, perhaps enough to sustain them through the school year? I could get on Uncle Dennis' crew!" she said. Uncle Dennis was not her real uncle but instead my childhood lifetime friend who was Superintendent of the Laguna Hotshots. Dennis was an El Cariso Hotshot with me at the start of his career too. Well "Yes," I said "But!!!"

Wendy played water polo in high school (with the boys) and was a swimmer in multiple events including the 500 meters. She was in very good shape, "but" hotshots go far beyond that. And yes, in a good fire season you can make some good dough, "but" it is not guaranteed, and fire season actually bleeds into both semesters, making school somewhat difficult to complete. And once I engaged in wildland firefighting I never returned to college. And the last big "but" (notice only one "t" on the but) had to do with feminine hygiene! Honey I said, "I think you have the will to handle the physical aspects of hotshots! But can you handle pooping in the woods and worse yet having your monthly girl thing on the fireline?" She gave it some serious thought and decided she absolutely could do it and wanted to give it a go. And yes, she did end up on the Laguna Hotshots, with a little nepotism, albeit fake nepotism, used to help her get hired. She stayed with it and succeeded 100% on her own efforts. She later moved to the Stanislaus Hotshots and worked her way up to Division Chief on the Stanislaus National Forest. Proud Daddy? You think? Absolutely!

Joel, my number two son didn't really want much to do with college. He was an average to slightly above average student with no desire to pursue school beyond high school graduation. He was athletic, a heck of a good wrestler and ballplayer. He was somewhat like me as far as thinking of going Forest Service right out of high school. Joel got hired his first summer out of school on a wildland Fire Engine Crew. Not a hotshot, but a great experience as well. It didn't take long for him to get the hotshot bug! Well, God bless Uncle Dennis (that again would be fake Uncle Dennis) as Joel was hired or basically transferred to the Laguna Hotshots. After one season with Laguna, I kind of inadvertently got in his stuff. I was promoted to Division Chief of the District Joel and the Laguna Hotshots were on. A Forest Service rule prohibits him from being in my direct line of supervision, so he had to move. Perhaps a string was pulled, I will never tell, but he was transferred to the El Cariso Hotshots. He too has had a great career and is currently a Fire Engine Captain on the Cleveland National Forest. Needless to say I am very proud.

And last but certainly not least, my stepson Jesse. Jesse struggled some in High School and beyond for a couple of years experimenting as we do and basically lacked real good direction. But on his own he came to me and expressed interest in getting some stability in life and inquired about the Forest Service and/or firefighting in general. Well things had changed some in recent years and "who you know" didn't carry the weight it used to. Hiring was more limited, and you had to have some special qualifications or education to be competitive. Jesse enrolled on his own into a Wildland Fire Academy at a local Community College. He gave it his all and successfully completed the program adding to his resume his certification as a Wildland Firefighter, making him very reachable for seasonal fire hiring. He landed a spot on the Descanso District fire engine crew. This was the District I had retired from and yes, Uncle Dennis was still there at that time. That aside we were so proud he had done everything required to land the job. And a couple of years down the road he became a Laguna Hotshot! Am I a proud dad? Well of course as my heroes have always been hotshots; Wendy, Joel, and Jesse are my heroes!

Life in a Nutshell

Despite the rigorous training and the vast fire experience gained by virtue of continual involvement in most of the nation's largest and most devastating wildfires, hotshots are not exempt from tragedy! Prior to my start with El Cariso, on November 1, 1966, the crew experienced tragedy on the "Loop Fire" on the Angeles National Forest in Southern California. When the fatal accident occurred El Cariso had been attempting to connect a fireline about 200' long downhill towards a Los Angeles County Fire Crew working up toward them. This was planned to be the final action necessary to control the fire. Unaware they were located at the top of a chimney or chute (a topographical area that can funnel and force fire rapidly uphill similar to a fireplace), a sudden flare-up occurred placing them in immediate unforeseen danger. This resulted in the immediate death of 10 members of the crew, 2 additional deaths later in the hospital, and serious injury to most of the remainder of the crew. Lessons learned from this horrific tragedy have likely saved hundreds of lives going forward. Very official and rigid requirements for downhill fireline construction were established that make it safer for all involved in wildland fire suppression as a result of the Loop Fire.

Although sadly there have been others, I want to share briefly about one additional hotshot fire tragedy. The Granite Mountain Hotshots were a proud group of firefighters. They were the only municipal hotshot crew in the nation, established and managed by the city of Prescott, AZ. All other hotshot crews were federally sponsored by the Forest Service, Park Service, Bureau of Land Management or Bureau of Indian Affairs. This crew worked extremely hard to fulfill all the requirements necessary to be deemed a Type 1 Hotshot Crew. It was no easy task as the training was provided primarily by the Feds and it complicated things considerably. But they did it and deserved their Type 1 rating. On June 28, 2013 the crew was assigned to the Yarnell Incident in the mountains just south of their home base in Arizona. It was a lightning caused fire, not particularly unusual for that time of year in that area. Thunderstorms, although sometimes accompanied by rain, can produce terribly erratic and ferocious downdrafts (winds) that can increase fire intensity and alter the direction of fire spread.. On June 30th, the crew was in a safety zone within the perimeter of the fire (an area deemed to be safe from the existing dangers of the fire). The gusty winds kept fire active but not a threat to the crew at that time. From their vantage point it appeared that some structures (homes, barns, outbuildings) could be potentially threatened down at the bottom of the ridge and in a flat meadow type area. With the existing fire conditions, a decision by the Superintendent was made to leave the safety zone and walk through the unburned vegetation ahead of the fire to get to the structures to provide protection should the fire pick up and seriously threaten the structures. There could have very well been a life threat as well, as it was unknown if there were any people still in or about the structure area. His apparent determination assumes that he felt there was plenty of time to make this move safely. While walking through the brushy area to access the meadow below, heavy downdrafts increased the fire spread and intensity instantly. The crew was trapped in perhaps the worst possible place when this occurred. They were still too far from the bottom to make it there safely and too far down the hill to return to their safety zone. Air support was ordered immediately but due to radio problems the order was never completed, and confirmation of their exact location never took place. Their pre-established "lookout", a trained firefighter was on a high point where he could see what was going on and did his best to alert his crew to the sudden change. But all their actions were to no avail. The fire was moving too quickly. They deployed their fire shelters, laid prone on the ground under aluminum tents designed to provide some protection in the event of a burnover. Only it was too little and too late, and 19 firefighters were overcome by fire and lost their lives. The fire took the entire crew, leader and all, minus the one person serving as the "lookout" at a somewhat distant knob. This was one of the deadliest tragedies in the history of wildland firefighting. Needless to say, it was devastating to the entire nation, but certainly more so to the whole hotshot community! A major motion picture "Only the Brave" was made following this tragedy that fairly accurately depicts the events related to this incident. It is well worth viewing but bring a tissue or actually a box of tissue!

As I wind this chapter up I want to conclude with a brief description of my first fire as a hotshot and then share the life lessons I was fortunate enough to gain from my experience in this role. My first fire was the Safety Harbor fire on the Wenatchee National Forest in the state of Washington. I was an El Cariso Hotshot from Southern California. This fire was an incredible experience. Fresh out of high school and having just completed my basic firefighter training we were dispatched to Washington, thousands of miles away. Besides being my first fire experience, this fire was in a state

I had never been to. What an experience. It was a timber fire in a beautiful or should I say stunning setting off of Lake Chelan in central Washington. We flew to Washington on an airplane which was also a first for me. My life was changing rapidly. We were shuttled in a bus to fire camp. Fire camp is for all practical purposes a mobile city. Sometimes, within hours but certainly within a day or two, a base of operations is established that somewhat mirrors a small town. There are kitchens, tables, chairs, supplies, food, sleeping facilities, showers, restrooms, and even a commissary. And this is done in highly remote areas. I was certainly impressed! On our very first shift I got to fly in a helicopter, another novelty in my life. To get to this helicopter we had a nice boat ride around and across a portion of the lake. People would pay good money for a boat tour such as this. All these new experiences and I had yet to engage in my first firefight, breathe smoke, or help produce even one inch of fireline. Timber fires have a certain glamour to them in the fire world and Safety Harbor had it all; ground fire, crowning, and spot fires. It was a very active first fire with fire running along the ground, climbing up into the tree canopy, and sending embers far ahead of itself starting additional fires and increasing its spread. I was extremely pleased with the confidence I had in our leadership or I would have surely required a frequent change of fresh undergarments on multiple occasions. Well the glamour dissipated rapidly as the hikes increased, the heat took its toll, and the work seemed torturous and endless. It wasn't long before I was seriously questioning the hastiness of my decision to pursue this potential career of wildland firefighting. On multiple shifts we walked 6 hours just to get to our starting point for work and then worked 12 -16 hours after that. And then at shift's end we would walk back out to where we started, dead tired. As we neared the completion of our 15-day assignment the drudgery was winning over the novelty. I remember thinking my first fire could very well be my last, as resignation from this craziness was the only sensible solution. We had boiled meals in a bag and went days without a shower. Sixteen to eighteen hour shifts and sometimes longer with very little sleep needless to say. As the fire ended it seemed my poor attitude began to end as well. On the journey home I started to notice my focus was less on the trying times of the previous two weeks. It changed quickly to celebration of the good times and the glamour of firefighting. No longer was it, "I quit"! Instead exclaiming how I had successfully put out my first major forest fire! Admittedly others did help to put it out as well. But I got to fight fire in God's country, and we won! I was part of an incredible well-oiled machine that played a very important role in beating back the beast. Amazing sometimes how easily we forget the drudgery and hold on to the charm of a situation! That certainly works for me.

***

So, what did hotshots do for me? First and perhaps most significant, I learned a lot about being a "Teamwork"...my character attribute for this chapter. Camaraderie is working together as a team, in community, in fellowship, both on and off duty. Each part of the hotshot machine was required to effectively perform our duties and responsibilities and all on an equally important basis. This attribute of "Teamwork" led to a tremendous trust, that was required in the dangerous situations in which we were sometimes placed. I learned too about tenacity, the ability to go on when you think you cannot. That was a frequent occurrence especially on long shifts or particularly long assignments. It provided me with strength of purpose and improved my overall determination. I learned to just place one foot in front of the other and keep repeating the process until the mission was accomplished. Another thing I think I learned on the Hotshots was that I knew very little overall, not only about fire but about life and I needed to know much more. The more I understood fire and its behavior, the more I discovered what I didn't know. But learning about it was critical for my own safety and for the safety of others who put their trust in me. My experience was overall very adventurous and fun, kind of a sick fun, but nonetheless fun. So, I guess I learned how to make good out of adversity and find enjoyment in some of the tougher experiences in life. I learned a lot about pride, the good pride not the bad! I am proud that I was a hotshot. I am proud I was an El Cariso Hotshot. I am proud of my children who were hotshots (and certainly proud of my other kids too!). I am proud of all of those who have given their life for others by serving as hotshots. I am proud of every hotshot crew out there and the good they are still to do. There is likely no better team in this world than a well-oiled team of Hotshots. Did I mention, "My heroes have always been hotshots"?

If The Grass Seems Greener
Contentment

CHAPTER 3

"My wife and I laugh about how competitive we can be, but please know I laugh more"

We live in a competitive world! Agree? Everything is a competition. Even childbirth; I am going to have a boy for sure. Or I am going to have a girl, I know this time. I am going to have it by this date or that. I am going to keep my weight down during my pregnancy, this time for sure. We have it in family. I have to outperform my siblings or please mom or dad more. I want to go further in life or excel more than them. We compete in school. Grades and report cards are the breeding ground for competition. We grow up with competition piercing us from every angle. Sports are competition! Dating and romance somehow has evolved to a competition. Work is major competition. Do your best to get that promotion, work harder to make more scratch. Beat your associate or even your friend out of the upcoming overtime. Even in our Church, let's be a better church, such and such church is doing this so we should be doing more. Competition is rampant in our life! So, is it completely a bad thing? I don't believe by nature it necessarily is. It has inherent value that is critical to our growth as a person. We need to care about the birth of our child and how we express it is not really an issue. We need to try hard to succeed both within and outside our family and be a strength to each other. Trying our best in school is actually a real quality character trait. And sports wouldn't exist without competition right, wrong, or indifferent. And our church; certainly, we should care about doing things better...but not necessarily because some other church might be. So, I believe healthy competition is a good thing, but again I am just one of life's biggest self-proclaimed nuts so what do I know? So, what's the downside of competition if there is one? I think there just might be! I think there is a point when competition embattles or interferes with our contentment and contentment can be one of life's most treasured values. Self-satisfaction in who we are is an incredible accomplishment in life and certainly a valiant goal for anyone to strive. A balance between our competitive nature and our need for contentment is critical.

    I have been what I call a "hitter" all of my life. I pretty much go after it! Now that might sound a touch boastful but really it is not all good, so not actually boastful at all. I was a hitter on the bad things in my life as well. I wanted to be the best firefighter on the planet and likewise I hit the drug life equally hard with all I had. I considered myself to be highly competitive by nature as well as a grass was always greener kind of guy! If things looked better elsewhere, I usually went for it. Note the past tense in the last sentence. I like to think I am in an overall better place today. As far as being competitive, I believe I now have better discernment for healthy competition versus damaging or burdensome competition. I draw much better lines and boundaries then ever in my past. And the grass being greener, I have learned this important life lesson. Yes, the grass can in fact be greener on the other side, but there is another option besides taking a giant somewhat blind leap over the fence to get to that luscious grass! If the grass seems greener elsewhere I may just need to water my own grass. I may need to apply fertilizer or other nutrients to my side of the fence. I may just need to provide greater care for my lawn or pasture and soon thereafter admire the beautiful change in my life. So, more about me and greener pastures!

Chapter 2 addressed in depth my time as a "hotshot" in the U.S. Forest Service. After my first two years on the hotshots I was transferred to a Fire Engine crew as the Engineer or basically the vehicle operator and second in charge of the crew. Advancement in the Forest Service was usually aided by diversity in work experience, so it seemed to be and was a good move. Being promoted into this position with only limited hotshot experience rewarded my work ethic I spoke of earlier. There was a lot to learn in my new position; Engine Operation, Pumps & Hydraulics, Hose lays or water delivery, and the responsibilities involved with my new supervisory role. On the Captain's days off I was completely in charge of the crew and responsible for their safety as their supervisor. This was not just for station activities but in the event of a wildfire too. I went from being a head down line cutting hotshot to a position with incredible responsibility. I had to make decisions on fires with regard to how we would attack the fire, what additional resources would be needed, and more. It was overwhelming at times, but I really seemed to like to be put in that position.

My next move just a year later was to Fire Prevention Technician. This was another complete change from my previous three fire seasons. First I became a full-time employee with yearlong work and no longer a seasonal. I was in a position where I was somewhat my own boss and patrolled the forest with an emphasis on fire prevention. This job had a law enforcement component as well as a strong public education component to it. It was interesting and I still was able to respond to fires in our area. It did lack the team element that I so cherished during hotshot and Engine Crew assignments.

So again, the following year I moved on. I was selected to be the Engine Captain in charge of a fire engine and crew. This was another promotion and now I was the primary supervisor and leader for a 7-person crew. Things were looking pretty good for me in the dream career I had revered since my youth. My station was referred to as an "out" station or basically off the beaten path. That was opposed to a station located on or adjacent to a primary highway or major road. It had its advantages for sure. Our Chiefs didn't visit nearly as often as they did at other stations, so we were on our own a lot. The remote nature for me just increased my admiration for my job and its work environment. We had a good crew and accomplished a lot of good work both on and off fire incidents. In fact, I had a bet with my Chief that my crew could finish this pretty major fuelbreak project in a month's time, if we were not taken away too often by fire assignments. He said if we did we could play pinochle the rest of the fire season and not be required to do anything else but our basic daily tasks. It was a great challenge and we did it! Only thing is my crew were such conscientious workers we actually continued other projects anyway and pretended to play pinochle when the Chief came out to our station.

Again, my next year involved a promotion. I was selected to be the El Cariso Hotshot Crew Superintendent. My absolute dream job within my dream career! I was in charge of a 30-person crew (2 fifteen-man squads) and one of the top crews in the nation at that. My immediate reaction was that this will be my job the rest of my career, which at that time would have been anywhere between 25 -30 years. Career long Hotshot Superintendents were rare across the country as Sup's, as they were called, were clearly good candidates to move up in the chain of command to the Battalion Chief level and beyond. But those who spent 20 plus years as a Superintendent were legends within the Fire Service and I just thought I might want to be a legend too.

To this point in my career I could not have asked for a better outcome. I went from first year hotshot, Engineer, Fire Prevention, Engine Captain and now Hotshot Superintendent. Not a single thing could have made my career to date any better. My world at work was awesome. At home many positive things existed as well but not totally without issue. I had a good wife, 3 beautiful children, and a very comfortable home. But for starters the career itself presented a challenge to home life. In a busy fire season, we can be gone over 200 days. This is a good portion of a year that you are not doing an appropriate share of the home responsibilities. It is very similar to the difficulties for families in military service. On top of that, partying and celebrations were common both on and off fire assignments. Sadly, I did more than my share of the revelry. So, in addition to being away for fires, I was also gone often with the crew celebrating our heroics. It affected my marriage certainly, but to this point time it was still somewhat manageable.

Then I experienced the first bummer of my still blossoming career. In August of 1978 well into my first fire season as Superintendent, Congress had instituted a major reduction in funding for the U.S. Forest Service and other government agencies with fire suppression responsibilities. Not a new problem within the government but this time it was a pretty drastic cut in funds requiring some serious actions. The Forest Service in their infinite wisdom decided to make it all up by cutting 50 hotshot crews nationwide, affectionately known as the "Hotshot Massacre of 1979". This cut was shared across the forests throughout the country and one crew was to be removed from the Cleveland National Forest where we resided. Initially upset by this senseless government faux pas, I was confident my crew would not be the one selected to shut down and disband. After all we were the legendary El Cariso Hotshots. We were one of the original "Interregional" crews. We had a rich history. We had exemplary performance ratings on incidents whereas others on the forest couldn't always make that claim. Geographically if the forest was to lose a hotshot crew it would likely come from the middle to provide coverage from both the north and south on the forest. And we were the crew on the north end. All logic made me certain we would survive the massacre. WRONG! El Cariso was selected to disband out of simple convenience. On our District was a vacant Battalion Chief position which I was qualified for and was moved into. There were two vacant Captain positions on the District and my two foremen were moved into those spots. They took care of the "supervisory overhead" but did virtually nothing for the crew. Palomar Hotshots in the middle of the forest had a couple of openings that were filled by a couple of our crewmembers. Most, however, were just laid off and not placed in another position. So, at least for that time El Cariso Hotshots no longer existed.

Essentially I had the perfect career with the exception of this one minor bump! I say minor bump because although emotionally it was devastating, the end result was me being promoted to Battalion Chief. Our District had three BC's. One supervised the north half of the District's Fire Stations, one supervised the south half of the District's Fire Stations, and the other supervised Fire Prevention and Law Enforcement within the whole District. All reported up to our District Division Chief. Between the hotshot massacre, the government funding deficit, and the forest's logic in selecting El Cariso as the crew to disband; I really struggled reconciling it all. That on top of the fact that our pay in general was falling considerably behind the municipal and state fire agencies each and every year. Our life began to suck some, or so I thought. The reality of the situation was I had it pretty darn good. Still it was hard to get past our crew disbandment. The competitive side of me wanted to know why us? Earlier in the year we had an investigation into our crew for an alleged hazing incident. An investigator from the Washington Office came and locked the crew in separate rooms after briefing my overhead team about the allegations. Their set-up prohibited the crew from linking their stories, and after the interviews and with further discussions we were cleared of the incident. The final report said something to the effect, "Although perhaps overzealous in their plight, the crew did not do any of the alleged actions claimed by the victim." Over, done deal. Nobody on the crew received disciplinary action. But to this day, I cannot help but feel that was the real reason El Cariso was selected to be the crew to disband.

Life goes on! I was BC North, Roger (a friend and former El Cariso Hotshot) was BC South, and Greg (also a friend and former El Cariso Hotshot) was BC for Prevention & Law Enforcement. We worked well together, and we grumbled well together. Because of our blend of responsibilities with fire and forest management, federal wildland firefighters were not necessarily recognized as full fledge firefighting personnel. This was evidenced in pay and other benefits when compared to others in the firefighting community. It wasn't all about pay and compensation for us, but it meshed with and amplified the other struggles such as the unstable funding and job security issues that didn't previously exist. Our "grass" was beginning to dinge and oh did it start to seem much greener on the other side!

I have always felt grumbling breeds more grumbling and it leads quickly to discontent. The reality of my situation was I had it pretty good with an unlimited future. I fell into that competitive and self-serving mode of "I deserve better, I deserve more". Well if there is strength in numbers Roger, Greg, and I became strong malcontents together! We didn't purposely stir the pot outwardly but within our group grew increasingly dissatisfied with our situation. Greg came in one day after receiving an estimate for some tree work at his home, amazed at the money they charge. Upon hearing this, Roger and I were as well. It only took moments to begin to piece together a plan for the three of us to enter the world of private enterprise. Oh yes, the grass was deep green on the other side and all three of us were ready to leap the proverbial fence. To our credit we did take some time to rationally think this over and investigate it thoroughly. We had the tree cutting skills from our Forest Service experience. We had no climbing skills but had a dear friend who was a rock climber. I am slightly embarrassed to write that we translated that into: with brief training from Gordon the rock climber we would all be able to climb trees. Between the three of us we had some administrative and management skills that would be similar to those required in this prospective business. So, in a nutshell (emphasis on nuts), we convinced ourselves we would have the talents and wherewithal to pull this off. Remember deep Ireland-like green grass on the other side! We were not stupid people and all equally aggressive and hard working. What we may have missed is the fact it would take a bundle of work and a bundle of money to fully support three families…each separately owning a home and all the financial obligation that goes with it.

So, picture this. Our Division Chief Marv is asked by us to meet with him to discuss something important on our minds. Now we got along very well with Marv, but the word "coup" had to enter his mind. Although certainly not a hostile takeover the three of us had never scheduled something of this nature before. We shared our plans to leave the Forest Service and go into business for ourselves and shared also what that business would be. We discussed our timeline which, as I recall, was basically shortly thereafter. Marv would lose his entire supervisory sub-staff very soon and all at once. Surprisingly he understood and kind of supported our thoughts and decision. He too had been disappointed with a lot of the goings on within the government. After some discussion Roger stayed on a little longer and didn't join us until later. But yes, we did leave our supervisor pretty shorthanded and "Too Tall Tree Service" was created. Too Tall was my nickname in the Forest Service obviously related to my limited stature. It just seemed an appropriate name for a tree business.

It didn't take long to realize exactly why those tree companies charge so much to trim or remove a tree. Within that price is at least a small stipend for the risk and danger involved. And because of that, liability insurance was exorbitant, and one would be foolish to operate without it due to the risk. The difficulty for disposing of the debris and the magnitude of the debris had certainly escaped us some, not to mention the dump fees. Most every piece of equipment required for the business was specialized, expensive, and demanded continual maintenance and/or replacement. Gas, oil, mechanical service on the vehicles, brush chippers, chain saws all added up to additional expense. It is not like all of this blew past us completely in our original planning, but we certainly didn't adequately appreciate the significance of it all.

We did learn quickly how to perform safely the bulk of the processes required to be effective in this line of work. It took a while to become competent in bidding and estimating correctly the cost of the jobs. Greg and Roger entered into the partnership in a better financial situation than me. In part because they each were married with working wives and no children and probably mostly because they were much better at managing money than me. Any working capital we entered into the partnership with dissipated faster than anticipated. We were doing good work when we had it, but still had a pretty good learning curve to overcome. The three of us were drinking buddies in the Forest Service and that picked up a lot once we had the freedom of being our own boss. It had its effects on the business, but truth be told mostly with me. My alcohol consumption had increased significantly over the years. Soon we would struggle to make ends meet. When the month end finances were insufficient, Greg and Roger graciously covered my compensation first. That was an obvious blessing but tugged hard on my "pride" strings. It wasn't very long at all before discussions of the merits of our decision were questioned and on an increasing level. Roger and Greg both explored the possibility of returning to the Forest Service. I stubbornly thought we got this, and I was probably in the most vulnerable situation of us all. The green grass was eluding me, but I had no intention of giving up. Well Greg and Roger did. They didn't really give up; I know now that they made a very good life decision to cut their losses and move on.

Let me spin you through my next several years, some a review from Chapter 1. I beat my head against the proverbial wall for about 7 years. I went from my partnership with Greg and Roger to trying to continue it on my own. I struggled basically the whole time. I next convinced myself I could pull this off by moving it from Southern California to another state, Arizona. We sold our home and uprooted the family to move to Arizona. The cost of living assured me, at least in my mind, that we could make it there. Actually, I ended up with a lot of work, but it was in multiple locations throughout the state. I was on the road most of the time. Drinking and drug use was on the increase. My wife and kids were left alone in a strange location while I went up and down the state to make ends meet. I even took a multiple week big tree job back in California, again leaving them alone in Arizona. This led quickly to divorce and me still searching aimlessly for that green grass!

My wife and I split up and all of the family ended up back in Southern California. I continued to struggle with my livelihood and the drugs and alcohol. I had a second wife and fourth child detailed earlier. My downward spiral came graciously to an end that night in the camper when I called "BS" on my life.

***

The lesson for this chapter is easy. Although there is a plethora of mistakes from which to gain lessons one was clearly highlighted. When the grass is greener on the other side, you may just need to water your grass. My Forest Service career was not perfect, but it was very good with endless possibilities. Having your crew disbanded and landing a Battalion Chief job is not the end of the world. Minor issues at home, increased alcohol consumption, and a hurt feeling or two will not be resolved just by changing careers or moving to a new location. There is an old A.A. saying that wherever we go, there we are! At 68 years old I still face "greener grass" situations and sometimes it might be best to leap that fence, but I suggest that to be rarely. However, going forward, I plan to never let that be my decision without first considering what I can do to make my current situation better! My character trait for this chapter is "contentment". Contentment is the perfect neutralizer for that sometimes-harmful competitive nature the world unwittingly imposes upon us on a daily basis.

Never Stop Growing
Perseverance

> *"The best thing about the good old days is I was neither good nor old"*

OH, TO KNOW THEN WHAT I KNOW NOW! Have you ever said or thought that…or something remarkably similar? Well I certainly have many times. When we finally figure out life we are usually too old to do much about it or so it seems anyway. Perhaps this claim is mildly exaggerated, but it is not without considerable insight. When I look back on my life I would do so much of it differently if magically given the opportunity. Hindsight is 20/20 so they say and unfortunately it is pretty hard to change the past. But we can always change our attitude and direction going forward, no matter what phase of life we are in. Whether you are a teen, a young adult, or even a really old guy like me we can still make positive change anytime we put our mind to it. Our trials, our mistakes, and life difficulties can be an insurmountable weight on us if we let them be. We become frustrated and our frustration too often inhibits our growth and diminishes our God given right for stability, contentment, and happiness in our life. Oh, if I could do it over again I would not do this thing or say that thing or whatever! We dwell too much, too long on things we cannot change. It not only stunts our growth as a person, it robs us of so much potential joy both in the present and going forward in life.

I am <u>not</u> a trained and licensed Psychologist or even an educated life counselor. In fact, I have very limited post High School formal education. I have however been able to glean some very useful tenets and tools during my time here on earth. One thing in particular that I discovered is that life is a marathon and not just a huge collection of sprints or short races. I like to think of it as an ongoing ever-evolving process. If we think more about the long haul and less about the moment, it can really shape our thinking and help us manage life in a more productive way. If we understand that fully, we seem to handle life situations in a much more mature and competent manner. We become comfortable with the fact that our "bummers" in life are short lived and really just opportunities for growth. By keeping this mind set we can progressively become a more solid and complete individual as well as better understand the struggles of others.

I like the "process" theory. I believe that life is a continual process in which we can make mistakes, learn, change, and grow. My process idea is not rocket science; in fact, it isn't even really my idea at all. I think we innately understand our basic growth process. We are born into this world as infants, become toddlers, pre-teens, teens, young adults, adults, and then really old people…or seniors as they call us. I am kidding of course, maybe just a little about us seniors having no purpose. The process I am talking about however is our growth as a person internally. We start out with an abundance of instruction that helps us with life's basics. We receive guidance and assistance on the food we eat, how to walk, our communication skills, our learning abilities, our relationships and more. The world in which we live has orchestrated a generic path that the majority of us take to become somewhat productive adults at some point in our life. Sometimes it works and sometimes it does not. We are progressively educated, regularly assessed or evaluated, and may or may not get to advance to the next phase of our growth. In our humanity we have a strange propensity for ranking everything as different levels of performance or accomplishment. Although a mild motivator on occasion, it generally defeats its purpose by placing emphasis on our deficiencies. Once we truly appreciate the concept of life as a process, we can use life's difficulties to help us to become more responsible human beings.

I have yet to talk in much detail about my Christian faith but would like to now. First a short overview of my walk with Christ. As I alluded to earlier in this work, I attended church in my youth. Mom took us, dad did not attend, and it was a fairly regular life activity for me and my siblings. My personal relationship with God or any higher power was quite impersonal at best during this time. I believed in God as a distant being that may have even created all things, but not someone or something I could intimately relate to. He (or of course She) was kind of Wizard-like or a "Fairy God Father" type figure residing somewhere in outer space among the stars. It was really something that was completely outside of my realm of understanding. I guess I thought that Church and/or God taught basically good things, so it was worthy of my time and possible exploration. Although I did very little exploration. I never connected with any depth until much later in life.

My "come to Jesus" time of my life was detailed in an earlier chapter but happened at the height of my drug use and life desperation. Probably a fortunate time for me as I was in drastic need of something better. As a result, I was open for some much-needed change in my life. It opened so many doors that had been inadvertently shut unknowingly by me. Whether you are a believer or not, please know there are so many positive teachings and life lessons within Christianity that can work for anyone. The core values that I fell in love with were many, but I would like to discuss a few. First and foremost, finally for me, I gained a true understanding of love. I learned about unconditional love and love without end…something I hadn't really experienced to any large degree in my "worldly" days. I learned about compassion, really caring <u>about</u> others as well as caring <u>for</u> others. I learned about grace, forgiving others for imperfections so similar in nature to mine and understanding it was okay to be broken and at times inadequate. I experienced a peace inside of me beyond all understanding, to paraphrase some from the Bible. And I learned about hope, something I had very little of prior to this time. To borrow a clever cliché from the world of recovery, "I once was a hopeless drug fiend, but now I am a drugless hope fiend!" For me it was and still is Jesus that taught me this.

So, how does any of this relate to the process of life? My savior now is no longer a distant "Wizard" that waved a wand and made the world happen. He is someone who loves me intimately and helps me grow daily. He has grown me through His teachings and His Word. Early in my newfound walk with Jesus I latched on to some verses that identify a valuable life process, that to this day continues to give me indescribable hope. This scripture; *2 Peter 1: 5-9* goes something like this: *"For this very reason, make every effort to add to your faith goodness; and to goodness, knowledge and to knowledge, self-control; and to self-control, perseverance; and to perseverance, godliness; and godliness, mutual affection; and to mutual affection, love. For if you possess these qualities in increasing measure they will keep you from being ineffective and unproductive in your knowledge of our Lord Jesus Chris. But whoever does not have them is nearsighted and blind, forgetting that they have been cleansed from their past sins."*

There is a lot of Christianese in this and of course there is, it is scripture! But there is a lot of common sense as well, if you happen to struggle with Christianity or other faith-based beliefs. In a nutshell, (the overall theme of this book) it diagrams a process that will guarantee to lead us to a better life, a life of hope and eventual contentment! So, let's examine this in detail looking at it from a faith-based perspective as well as a secular or worldly view. The scripture starts with an assumption that we begin with the core value known as faith. In the case of Christianity, faith is confidence in what we hope for and assurance about what we do not see, most particularly Jesus. Non-Christians have faith too, in multiple things. Most everybody believes that "wind" exists even though none of us have ever seen it. We have seen the results of it; the dust in the air and the swaying of the trees, so we without difficulty acknowledge its existence. We have faith the sun will rise, and the moon and stars will most likely appear in the sky. Faith is something we all need as a basic step of humility; acknowledging where we actually stand in the big scheme of things, no matter our personal beliefs. So, let's begin our process. Given the initial faith we started with we are asked to add to it goodness. Goodness is something we all easily accept as a treasured characteristic. Even if we struggle daily with being good, we somehow always have an appreciation for goodness and desire it in our lives. Next we add in knowledge, an irreplaceable attribute for growth of any kind, be it secular or faith based. Increasing our understanding of the world around us can be an enriching and edifying experience. Knowledge is then followed by self-control, a key player in managing our behavior in a positive way. I have been stuck on this one personally for some time. Although I believe I have continually improved, it is an area that takes my absolute best efforts to conquer. For that reason, I appreciate that all of this is a lifelong process and not an immediate requirement to be successful. It is next suggested that we focus on perseverance. I've tried that, but I just keep giving up! Just kidding, maybe a little. It is hard to keep going when the going gets tough, for me or most anyone. Keeping a "marathon" frame of mind can help us push through those times of struggle. Not that a marathon is remotely easy, but again it reminds us we are in for the long haul and not for a series of short sprints! It is then recommended to add a dose of godliness to our life. That sounds particularly religious but not necessarily unique to the faith-based community. Godliness can equate to transcendence leading to greatness, excellence, and possibly even perfection. We can all use a little of that! Continuing on we add to our evolving process mutual affection, also known as brotherly love. This is compassion, the caring for others or putting others first. We live in a me first world (to be discussed in great detail in a later chapter) making this a somewhat unnatural trait. But with work this can be one of the most rewarding changes we will ever experience in our life. And lastly and certainly not least is LOVE! The reference here is about perfect love. That being, love without conditions or requirements that is freely shared with all others and not a select few only. It is never-ending love, not short term or intermittent. Back to Christianity for a brief moment. Jesus when asked what he considered to be the greatest commandment he replied (in paraphrase form), "Love your God and love others!" For me a simple summation of what is required of us or once again "in a nutshell". So, I am not quite done with this train of thought. The verse concludes with the direction to possess these qualities in increasing measure and you will not be ineffective or unproductive. This thought thrills me! It implies that I am, and it is okay to be, a work in progress. I do not have to nail it from the beginning. During the process of my growth I can and will be increasingly more effective and productive. I can work towards being a better person. I will experience small successes…and success breeds success. The evangelist and teacher Oswald Chambers when reflecting on his thoughts from *2 Peter* says, "No one is born either naturally or supernaturally with character; it must be developed. We have to form Godly habits on the basis of the new life God has placed within us." So, person of faith or not, we must understand we are a continual work in progress and personally that sure takes a lot of pressure off of me!

So more about me. Sorry! I shared in Chapter 1 that earlier in my life I possessed some very positive traits and I had some not so positive ones as well. This of course is no different than most people. As I reflect back though I think for the longest time I was just who I was and that was it. I wasn't much different as a person overall, the same today as yesterday. This feeling reflected the bulk of my early life into my thirties and not just for a brief period of time. Not that I was all bad or required immediate reconstruction, but I was essentially stuck or very accepting of who and what I was...good, bad or indifferent! There was limited or no real growth in my life and things that don't grow wither and eventually die. I didn't fully recognize this, but I definitely felt or sensed it to a compelling degree. I desperately needed the means to increase who I am in a productive way. For me, my faith journey provided such an opportunity. Again, without emphasis on the existence of an omnipotent power, the teachings and examples from my Christian walk allowed me to mature in ways I never imagined. I began to take baby steps forward, without that "all or nothing" fear of failure. I learned to celebrate my successes and to view my struggles as opportunities. This was a giant leap for me. I learned that wherever I was on the good-bad continuum of life, I just needed to move closer to good and further from bad with each passing day. There is no light switch to flip on to make me good but instead accept that it is a process to be taken slowly over time. I was fortunate in many ways. I have an addictive personality which contributed to my difficulties earlier in life. That same addictive personality has worked to my benefit since my redirection took place. Instead of hitting the drugs and alcohol with the veracity of an "addict", I was now engaging in really good things with that same fervor. I was able to begin to add to my faith in an increasing fashion the elements of goodness, knowledge, self-control, perseverance, godliness, mutual affection, and love. I joined a church and didn't just attend on a leisurely basis; I became a church-aholic. I attend most every week. I joined Bible Studies and attend small group meetings. I participate in mission work and homebuilding in Mexico. I teach weekly classes at a Christian Recovery Home and became a Board Member of the same organization. I kicked up my exercise activities to borderline fanatic. I ran marathons, half-marathons, and climbed the highest mountain peaks in Southern California. I have a firewood ministry for those who can't afford it or have the means to provide for themselves. I do projects for my elderly neighbors. Yes I know that will be me very soon. I promise this is not meant to be boastful in any way, but instead to illustrate the positive use of my addictive nature. Most importantly is not the "stuff" I do, but more about what has happened to my heart. I have whittled away at that instinctive self-serving desire and have a keen appreciation when I am able to put others first. I am overwhelmed by the grace shown me, in spite of me, making it easier to extend that same grace to others. I have become so much more aware of real love and live to share it as well as receive it. Needless to say, I still have a long way to go no doubt. I don't end a day without wishing I had done better. But when looking back at who I was 30 years ago and who I am today my progress is pleasingly evident. I don't remotely want to rest on my laurels as I want to be more effective and more productive... and to borrow from our A.A. partners in recovery, I will simply do this one day at a time.

***

    This chapter covered a plethora of potential traits that can help grow us immensely as individuals. I however have selected "perseverance" as the character trait of note. As life beats us about the head, or even in good times, it can be extremely difficult to keep on moving in a positive direction. I am not by any means recommending we beat our heads against the proverbial wall but instead recognize that things can always get better if we just persevere. If we temper our expectations for life we can more easily remain motivated to grow and prosper. If we acknowledge that today is in fact a miniscule portion of life's entirety, our lows fizzle in strength to the point of extinction. Instead of dragging us down or holding us back, we can put them behind us and move forward in a self-edifying way. Perseverance builds character!

Mefirstness
Compassion

CHAPTER 5

"Sometimes I wake up grumpy and sometimes I let her sleep!"

Several years ago, I was asked to give the message at an upcoming church service as I have done occasionally in the past and still do periodically today. At that time there had been a nagging tug on my heartstrings that I just couldn't shake. What makes inherently good people get along so poorly and at times care so little for each other? I thought about it first at its most basic level...husband and wife, parent and child, friend to friend, and even just casual acquaintance to casual acquaintance. These are people that should in most cases have an innate love or caring feeling for the other. Yet there can still be explosive times in our relationships and total disregard for each other's situation or needs. So often this leads to complete severing of close relationships and a world too full of struggling people. Sadly, nobody ever wins, most everyone loses. This isn't just happening to other people, like those guys, her or him, did you hear about so and so, etc. It happens to everyone to one degree or another, even you and me. And then this same disease escalates to a higher level to include families, communities, whole countries, and even the world. And that can evolve into horrid conflicts, even World Wars or millions of people living at or below the poverty level. It happens in the secular environment as well as within the faith-based community. No one is exempt. It just doesn't make any sense as we all have a basic need to live in community. We need each other. Synergy is strength. Harmony with others brings peace to our hearts. Love conquers all. No one enjoys volatility in their life. There just isn't any good reason we should behave like this, it does nobody any good. But we do and we do so frequently. It is the rule and not the exception, so why is that? What makes us be contemptuous when our heart desires the complete opposite? What makes us selfishly care for ourselves first and avoid others of greater need? If I could answer these questions my book would certainly sell millions! That's not going to happen. While I do not pretend or begin to think I have the answer, I may have scratched the surface regarding the problem. It seems to me the root of every conflict is that one or more parties are not getting their way. From the argument I had with my loving wife last night to Pearl Harbor and the initiation of World War II. This might seem especially elementary, but I think that's okay. No sophisticated solution in the past has led to any kind of resolution or lessening of the problem. A deeper examination of these situations will reveal that one side or even both sides believed they were being violated and their personal violation must be rectified. In other words, I have been hurt and this needs to be made better! We want what we want for ourselves, rarely contemplating or considering the needs of others. We have a very self-centered nature overall. It's all about me!

So back to my message for church, what should I speak on? And then it hit me, so much of the conflict and distress in the world is a direct result of "MeFirstness". So, I committed myself to studying and sharing about this topic. Now, to my knowledge, I made that word up or at least I had never heard it before. I think it adequately describes our propensity to put ourselves before others. So once again in a nutshell, I believe it is MeFirstness that is truly the scourge of the earth. The argument I had with my wife last night was because one or both of us thought only of "me" first, although in our case it was most often me for sure. Even the poverty in the world directly relates back to MeFirstness. The homeless situation, MeFirstness. And I contend even the cause of World War II is rooted in MeFirstness if you take a very close look at it. So yes, I did do an entire sermon on "MeFirstness". And now I am devoting an entire chapter to it, as recognizing and understanding this disease could be the first step in resolving it, at least on a personal level. It has certainly helped me deal with much of the conflict in my life.

It is hoped that my examples and discussions to follow are not cause for debate as they are simply my thoughts and understanding for each of the situations as they relate to the concept of MeFirstness. They are mostly broad overviews and not necessarily historical representations of the facts in each case.

From the beginning of time, at least in the Christian tradition, MeFirstness has played a major role in the good and evil of mankind. Adam and Eve had it going on, their life was good. They were created from dust and landed in the Garden of Eden. Now I don't know about you but from dust to some beautiful and exotic garden seems like a pretty fortunate stroke of luck to me. Adam then receives some instruction of which most was highly favorable to their situation, should they follow it. He coughs up a rib and poof he is joined by Eve. It starts out very well. He and Eve are innocent and completely comfortable in their nakedness and their situation. I know I could be comfortable in their nakedness and their situation. But then along comes the serpent, oh the evil and tempting serpent. The serpent deceives Eve and she has a choice to make. A choice that can serve all people well for an eternity or just her and her alone for a very brief time. Unfortunately thinking only of herself, she eats the fruit from the forbidden tree. As a result, MeFirstness is responsible for basically all of the evil in the world, if of course you prescribe to the Adam & Eve story… and if not I have numerous other examples to share with you!

I subscribe to the theory that every war that has ever happened is rooted in some form of MeFirstness. Generally that is easy to say and would likely be supported to some degree by most. But let's look more specifically at a few just to strengthen my case.

Perhaps one of the most tragic wars in my mind was the Civil War right here in the United States. There have certainly been more destructive wars and we will talk in depth about one of those too. But the Civil War came so close to totally annihilating our country. It pitted brother against brother, family against family, and could have potentially ended everything our nation was and ever stood for up until that point in time. The cause could certainly be debated but I would like to speak to Pulitzer Prize-winning author

James McPherson's thoughts on this as shared in *A Brief Overview of the American Civil War*. McPherson speculates that, "the Civil War started because of uncompromising differences between the free and slave states over the power of the national government to prohibit slavery in the territories that had not yet become states." Individually we could easily reason from his statement that slavery was the cause of the Civil War. Or we could possibly pull out of this that major "differences" between the two sides was really the root cause. One might also surmise that "law" issues were the trigger or perhaps the question of power of the government might be. Not me, I am going to hang my hat on one word within his summation as the actual cause of the Civil War and that is the word "uncompromising". This is not to imply that those against slavery should have necessarily caved or relented to those who supported it. I don't think that is what compromise is. Merriam-Webster defines compromise as a settlement of differences by arbitration or consent reached by mutual concessions. To be uncompromising is basically taking the stand it is "my way or the highway" which is divisive and unproductive. To be compromising is to see the issue from the lens of the other and where appropriate make concessions that can lead to resolution of conflict. Once again resisting that natural tendency towards MeFirstness and putting the needs and concerns of others as a constant priority is the solution. In my mind, thinking ownership of another human being as a basic right is very self-serving to say the least. To view another of God's creation as inferior to us reeks of self-centeredness. I can only imagine how much could be resolved if we simply put the needs of others ahead of our own all of the time.

World War I was one of the most catastrophic conflicts in the history of mankind. My research shows military and civilian deaths are estimated between 15 -19 million with another 23 million casualties. It also suggests dozens of potential causes or issues that were at least in part related to the initiation of the war. One source labeled the following as collectively leading to this historic event: Alliance, Imperialism, Militarism, and Nationalism. Now I don't want this to be a brain strain history lesson so I will be brief. Alliance is simply partnerships formed by various entities based on mutual needs, concerns, and strengths. Imperialism was based on the need or desire to increase power and/or wealth. Militarism is organized and at times aggressive defense against potential foes or enemies. Nationalism focuses on one's own nation's support and promotion of its own interests. If we look at each of these closely there is an immediate connection to my theory of "MeFirstness". Alliances are generally formed when potential partners want to seek to get their own personal needs met by aligning with allies and generally it is done at the expense of those who oppose you. If alliances were instead made with more than just allies, it might work better to fully consider and meet the needs of all. Imperialism is all about power and wealth. Power and wealth are all about procuring all that I possibly can and is always at the expense of others. Imperialism is an incredibly self-centered focus. Although a case can easily be made for the need for military protection, militarism still at its core is protection of my stuff. It is usually in direct conflict with the needs and desires of the whole. Even though it is genuinely necessary, it is still very self-serving. So again, Hal suggests the real cause of World War I…basically MeFirstness! World War II much the same!

My two divorces, you guessed it MeFirstness! I shared briefly my story in Chapter 1 but quickly again only as it applies to this topic. An outsider looking in would have imagined my first marriage to be straight out of a fairy tale. I married my high school sweetheart, had 3 beautiful children, had a career that others would envy, and owned a comfortable home at a very early age. We had it all or at least we thought we did. Drinking and partying, mostly me though my wife joined in some, grew to be the rule and not the exception. I have since come to find out that most addictive behavior is clearly rooted in MeFirstness. Some folks may be more predisposed than others but regardless it usually doesn't take hold of our life until we drink the MeFirstness Kool-Aid! During the initial stages of our use we manage to keep it somewhat "social" in nature. We do that because we are still capable of thinking of and putting others before yourself. I will only drink this much because my wife thinks I am quite annoying beyond that point. I will limit my consumption because I am the designated driver for tonight and my friends are counting on me. I always insure I spend quality time with my children and make adult parties a very occasional event. We put boundaries into our social actions because we truly care about the thoughts, concerns, and needs of others. However, as our social drinking moves into the abuse stages we clearly experience a downward trend in the placing of other's needs ahead of our own. I certainly know I did! Incrementally my care and concern for others dissipated to a point I am embarrassed of today. My actions brutally hurt people I loved, yet I continued thinking only of Hal first and foremost. My second marriage and subsequent divorce was drenched in substance abuse by both my wife and me. Our relationship was essentially a comedy featuring two people mired in MeFirstness! It was not her fault more than mine. There was no, "if only she would…" It was two people neck-deep in a pool of self-centeredness with no viable way out as long as we continued to drink and abuse drugs. Speaking only for me, it was my first unselfish realization that I needed to do something immediately to get my daughter out of this situation that began my turnaround. I had battled for years thinking primarily of myself only before a simple unselfish thought changed my whole life.

Now changing gears for an additional look or consideration about MeFirstness not particularly related to conflict. 41 MILLION AMERICANS FACE HUNGER EVERY DAY not to mention how many worldwide. Estimates are close to a billion go to bed hungry across the globe. Yet the world produces 17% more food per person today than 30 years ago. Please worry less about my facts and more about the absurdity of these estimates. So why is there so much hunger when there appears to be enough food? It might be because we as individuals take care of our own nutrition first, our family second, perhaps our closest friends next, and rarely go beyond that. Well I for one have more food than I need and the means to procure more. I think the vast majority of the world are not unlike me. There is plenty to go around, we just don't have the desire or think we have the wherewithal to make it happen. When a problem seems bigger than us apathy often wins out. My efforts seem fruitless due to the magnitude of the situation. That is when selflessness needs to kick in. If I can't help many, I can help a few. If I can't afford to purchase food, I can grow it or help distribute it. If I combine my efforts with the efforts of others it will make a difference. I can personally consume less and waste less too. Mother Teresa was just one person, although it probably helps to have God on your team. But, kidding aside she was an incredible impact in reducing world hunger. We can be too. We need a lot more of "themfirstness"! Don't worry this is the only time I will wander into additional new words of which I have made up. Continuing, a flagrant image of MeFirstness is also seen in homelessness and the lack of effort to help provide shelter for so many people in need.

***

If any of my thoughts resonate with you and you find yourself agreeing with some of what I shared here, you probably need help! Just kidding but only a little bit. You do need help, as do I. We all need to take our anti-MeFirstness meds, humble ourselves greatly, and put others in that spot they truly deserve to be in. The day we all put others first is the day the calamity ends and the true joy in life begins. Chapter 5-character attribute is "compassion". The dictionary definition for compassion is "concern for the sufferings or misfortunes of others". Simple and succinct directing us to love others as we love ourselves, putting others first. It has been my experience that following this simple life direction can be incredibly rewarding and initiate a dose of healing to an ailing society.

Ain't It The Truth
Honesty

CHAPTER 6

"When you stretch the truth watch out for the snapback!"

I was teasing my wife the other day as we watched the President of the United States, Secretary of State, and POTUS' personal attorney frantically trying to get their story straight with regard to the impending "Impeachment" hearings. I said to her that the press and others are just not being fair, expecting all those people to remember correctly all of the lies they had spewed forth over the last several years. Don't they know how difficult it is to remember what we said or what we said we did, if we in fact had made it up? Once we have left the realm of truth, recalling anything we said or did in the past becomes an increasing impossibility!

I have had my share of messes during my 68 years here on earth. Most of them were of my own doing and some flavored with the unselfish help of others. Many had insignificant consequences while others far greater. Messes were never my goal, destination, or life target, but that didn't stop me from initiating or promoting such unwanted chaos in my life. In reality my desire would have been to not include life messes as any real part of my day to day existence. Many factors contributed to each of these undesirable situations, but I now know that the majority of these had a root cause either directly or indirectly related to "truth" or lack thereof!

Roget's Thesaurus lists the following as synonyms for truth; they are fact, certainty, reality, actuality, veracity, verity, authenticity, genuineness, exactness, honesty, integrity, fidelity, and uprightness. That's a bundle of descriptors and definitions that vary slightly to describe the same basic thing. A close look reveals they have one distinct similarity. They are absolute in nature. It is a fact, or it is not. It is a certainty, or it is not. It is reality, or it is not. That is the same way it is with truth. It is the truth, or it is not! There can really only be one truth in any circumstance or situation, no matter how hard we try to hint otherwise. Our understanding of this concept of truth could really help to simplify our life. I believe dealing with only one reality has to be easier than sorting through a plethora of potential possibilities in any situation. Yet we struggle to do it. For some reason we have the propensity to live our life riddled with exaggerations, modified truths or half-truths (as they are affectionately called at times), as well as downright lies. We try to soften the consequences of our untruth with terms like "half-truths", exaggeration, or another very popular deflection…a little white lie. When half-truth in and of itself guarantees that at least a portion of our words and/or actions lack truth and include some form of deceit. Exaggeration by definition implies again that our words and/or actions also lack some truth. We too often validate what we do if there is a dose of truth within our actions or we simply include a truth component somewhere among them. We convince ourselves we have satisfied our responsibility for truth when in reality any splash of untruth soils the entire circumstance completely. I don't know about you, but for me dishonesty can complicate my life very quickly. I remember things I actually did or said much more easily than I can remember something I made up or lied about. The reason is obvious. There is only one thing to remember if it was the truth and an infinite amount of possibilities if it were not. I don't do so well remembering things if I made them up, but I rarely struggle to recall a truth that I had once told.

So, why is that? Is it our nature to lie or short-cut the truth, which by the way is not in any way the actual truth once we choose to take a short-cut? If we believe in the creation narrative in the Bible, a case could certainly be made for our propensity to stray from the truth…just ask Adam and Eve or investigate the venomous intent of the serpent. Almost immediately a perfect creation was polluted with a spattering of poisonous deceit. When a young toddler gets caught with their hand in the proverbial cookie jar, they seem to have an innate talent for conjuring up an immediate fairy tale of why what really took place is mistakenly not what it seems. And think of the enormous number of canines in the world with severe abdominal issues from all of the alleged "homework" they were accused of eating by lackadaisical teenagers looking for an excuse. How many late-night "working at the office" stories really took place at the Pub around the corner or worse yet the hotel with a pay by the hour rate? Did George Washington cut down that darn Cherry tree or didn't he? We live in a world where truth has too little value and yet it is an absolutely essential ingredient in life that we cannot live peacefully without.

So why do we lie? If I knew the exact answer I would be border-line brilliant, a claim for which I have never made. Once again I am only one of life's nuts sharing my thoughts with the few who might be interested. I do believe struggling with the truth is in fact somewhat innate to us, like it or not. I think also, however, that we do have the ability to overcome this natural tendency to deceive with the proper effort. I think we lie at times out of simple convenience, not fully ferreting out the potential consequences of our actions. I think we lie sometimes to avoid the truth, if the truth makes us uncomfortable or what we believe to be the truth requires too much of us. At times we lie to spare feelings of others or at least that is what we think at the time. Although this is perhaps the most compassionate of reasons, lying rarely produces a positive outcome. We lie too because we can just be flat insensitive to others. Me being sensitive here I used the term *Insensitive* as a kinder depiction for downright mean! We don't particularly like to be mean, but we are okay with being "insensitive". For whatever the reason, we likely never learned to appreciate the proper value of truth.

The following short story is fictitious with names, titles, and place of employment fabricated to protect anyone past or present in my life from thinking it is about them. I suppose though, if they do, it would be only because they have a strong personal connection to much of its content. So, once upon a time a very talented, attractive, and eager young executive was hired to continue to lead this well-established functioning business shortly after the retirement of their predecessor. Success was eminent as the company had operated in a smooth prosperous manner for decades. The company was stable with quality staff and other employees remaining. Its new leader, let's call him Rex, seemed skilled enough and was filled with new and innovative ideas. It seemed to be a can't miss situation with all things considered. Well not all things perhaps. The one shortcoming picked up on somewhat quickly by some and much more slowly by others was that new leader did not always speak the truth. Initially there did not seem to be blatant lies so much as just minor little fibs here and there…or false excuses for things that didn't go just right. These usually related to him acting as though he knew everything about the company's operation but got caught falling short. The company would have surely understood that he wasn't yet up to speed, rather than he invent a story. In lieu of admitting his shortcoming, he would usually throw someone under the bus by stating so and so told me the company has always done it this way. Also, Rex was very aggressive by nature, perhaps more than the hiring team anticipated. He had a lot of irons in the fire over and above all the established responsibilities that came with the job. Unfortunately, this was at the expense of pre-established work practices that were so important to the company. There was a buzz throughout the workforce, mostly questioning some of the initial tactics of their new leader. A handful of complaints went up the chain of command. Initially they were taken as growing pains within the new leadership but eventually required some action. A small group of sub-staff leadership met with Rex informally hoping to get things easily and quickly changed to move in a more positive direction. In the discussion it seemed as though Rex quickly brushed off each concern by placing the blame on misinformation he received or that some individual had misled him. He would try to get better information going forward but not knowing who was giving him accurate details was always his excuse. Again, still informal, it was suggested to Rex that he focus on the existing programs for now more than the different direction he seemed to want to go. Well needless to say this did not resolve the problems. Sadly, this was not because Rex did not possess the capabilities to make this happen, but instead because he lived outside the truth too readily. In the more formal handling of the situation Rex was given a written *Performance Improvement Plan* requiring him to do some things differently. In the meeting he again defended every accusation by identifying who really was the culprit, of course not true. Rex had no chance of making this work out as he lived outside the truth and did not really realize he did. He had incredible skills and potential, but Rex works there no longer!

The Bible says the "truth will set you free" and I think there would be significant secular agreement with that statement as well. This is an important attribute of truth. When we find ourselves bound and gagged by the trials of life it is only truth that can free us from the bondage. Generally rooted in our most distressing situations are lies and untruths that have weaved their selves inadvertently into our life, holding us hostage unknowingly. It takes absolute truth to unravel us from the messes we create all too often. Many times, the truth is not pleasant and in fact downright awful, but it will always have a cleansing effect on any situation. Another attribute of truth is that it eventually surfaces in spite of our sometimes-aggressive efforts to conceal it. We waste a lot of needless effort trying to hide or camouflage the truth when in reality it will most likely be revealed. Little do we know we are at the core of our grief and nurturing our trials by feeding them with lies instead of healing them with truth.

Why do we take it so lightly? Why do we so readily excuse it? Why do we in some cases encourage it? Maybe it is because it the most rampant disease in today's world and we flat just don't know how to handle it. Practice <u>truth</u> and uncomplicate your life!

***

Honesty is the character trait for this chapter. Honesty is not just about telling the truth it is much more about who we are as a person. Honesty goes hand and hand with integrity and having integrity is perhaps the most honorable display of our character. Although I am far from perfect, I want people to assume I am telling the truth every time I speak. Not because I deserve it but because every time I have spoken with them I told the truth!

We Are Family
Commitment

CHAPTER 7

(Where there's a will, there's a relative)

I opened my eyes and the first thing I saw was my wife's beautiful smiling face looking straight into my eyes and she was more incredibly beautiful than I even remembered. I could not believe what had just taken place in my life over the last 12 hours or so and I am sure neither could she!

One set of our grandchildren, the youngest ones 3 & 6 years old, live in New Jersey and we reside in California. It takes very intentional planning always to make sure we are an active part in their life and to enjoy them as they grow up. Our other five grandchildren live more conveniently closer to us and we are routinely more actively involved in their lives. We try to visit our son Wes, daughter-in-law Amanda, and Henry & Bonnie a couple times a year in New Jersey and they usually come to us another time each year as well.

Our most recent trip was scheduled for early October and it would allow us to celebrate Bonnies 3rd birthday (just a little late), Dolo's (my wife) birthday the day after we arrived, and Henry's 6th birthday slightly before the official date, as our return home was just before his actual birthday. This plan, though mildly complex allowed for some great celebration opportunity and quality time with our New Jersey gang. My wife put some icing on the proverbial cake by purchasing tickets for her, our son Wes, and me to visit the Baseball Hall of Fame in Cooperstown New York for 2 days in the midst of our trip. It was an action-packed trip, but doable, nonetheless.

We arrived in New Jersey safely with all systems go. Day 2 was Dolo's birthday and after much discussion we decided to celebrate it with the whole family going out to the Red Lobster located conveniently in their town, Toms River. It seemed elegant enough for my low maintenance wife, yet comfortable and kid friendly enough for our gang of six which included the two youngsters. Mid-afternoon I was relaxing some in Wes' recliner in their family room while Wes and Dolo were in his adjacent office attempting to book a rental car for our Cooperstown trip. We did not want to leave Amanda and the kids without a vehicle for two days while we were enjoying the Baseball Hall of Fame. Out of nowhere I began to feel a somewhat nagging pain in my jaw and thought it might be teeth related. It continued and seemed to increase in intensity as well as spread to my neck and into my upper arm and chest. Being a former EMT in my firefighter days I was aware of the symptoms of a heart attack or other heart related issue but did not want to go there just yet. Dolo came into the family room to get a question answered regarding the car rental and picked up immediately that something might be wrong. She asked and I shared that I was basically in the process of figuring that out. As the pain increased I laid down on the couch. Wes asked if we needed to go to Urgent Care and I asked for a moment to think this through. I wasn't opposed to Urgent Care but was quickly leaning towards 911 and more immediate help. After a brief moment, I asked them to call 911. The response was swift and thorough. A Toms River Police Officer arrived within minutes, followed by an EMT ambulance, and another Paramedic Ambulance. After a quick assessment they transported me to Toms River Community Hospital probably less than 10 minutes away. They gave me nitroglycerin to reduce the pain and monitored my heart in route. I received outstanding care from every one of them! At the hospital they immediately ran a series of tests to hopefully identify what exactly my issue was. I was confused because I am an avid hiker and exerciser who stays in pretty good shape always. The Emergency staff became confused as well because my chest x-ray, EKG, and blood work revealed nothing to point them in the right direction, yet I was in pretty consistent pain even with the nitro. A Physician's Assistant while explaining to us the dilemma of my test results, inquired about our recent flight from California just the day before. She thought it a possibility that a blood clot could have formed causing these same symptoms. She wasn't too confident but wanted to at least eliminate that possibility, so she ordered a CT Scan. At the completion of the CT Scan I was wheeled back into the Emergency Room to await the results. Dolo and Wes were by my side and my daughter Wendy was on the phone with me. My pain had increased to more unbearable levels. Shortly thereafter a Cardiologist, not my PA from earlier, came to talk with me. He said it was fortunate I had the CT Scan as it revealed not a blood clot, but instead an Aortic Dissection. He asked if I knew what that was. I said I know what each of the words mean but not what they mean together. He explained that the main artery going into my heart was basically splintered. I was bleeding into my heart…and this was a true emergency requiring immediate surgical repair. He said he had already ordered an air ambulance to take me north to New Brunswick to the Robert Wood Johnson Hospital. To my good fortune this is a world renown cardiac care hospital and upon my arrival they would perform immediate open-heart surgery. So, I was promptly loaded into a helicopter and it was about a twenty-minute flight to Robert Wood Johnson. Wes and Dolo drove an approximate hour plus to join me in the surgical preparation room with staff scampering around readying me and the facility for my surgery. By now it was after midnight. The surgeon was at an adjacent hotel catching just 20-30 minutes of sleep to prepare himself as he had a pretty exhausting day prior. Staff was under the instruction to call him just prior to start time and once I was fully prepped.

    Wes and Dolo made it to the hospital just prior to me going under the anesthesia and we were able to talk, pray, and cry some together prior to the surgery. I admittedly feared I might leave my honey for good or at least recognized the distinct possibility. We discussed it briefly but were jointly hoping for a completely different outcome. An attending nurse assured us I would be okay. The last thing I remember before going under was Dolo's pretty face and beautiful smile while she was holding my hand…and then absolutely nothing until I woke up to the same incredible face and thought to myself, "I made it" thank God! And I have this permanent vision of Dolo's smile, the first thing I saw upon waking up, that will be a constant strength to me the rest of my life!

I guess I was somewhat combative waking up and the nurse told Dolo that it made it impossible to remove the breathing tube to get me ready for the recovery room. I am told Dolores sternly but sweetly and again with that infectious smile calmed me down to a point where the nurse could perform his duties. During the course of all this my three older children Wendy, Mark, and Joel had decided to fly to New Jersey and be with us, what a blessing having them post-surgery and at my bedside during recovery. To this point everyone I had dealt with was outstanding. Doctors, nurses, emergency personnel were all courteous, efficient, professional, and comforting. My wife and Wes were both a strength for me the entire time. Wendy, Mark, and Joel showing up and being there for me was a God send. I was very confident my recovery was going to go great!

Little did I know at first that most of my recovery was going to take place in New Jersey. I knew I would spend a handful of days in the hospital recovery room but just assumed I would head back home to California immediately thereafter. Wrong! Remember that blood clot possibility from air travel thing? The Doctors would not let me fly for a month due to the potential of getting a blood clot on my return trip home. So, Wes and Amanda, "how do you like the thought of your parents living with you for an entire month?" Actually, they were extremely gracious and said we could stay as long as we needed, although I am pretty sure they prayed extra hard for a speedy recovery. I too would have periodic Doctor appointments in New Jersey prior to my official release home, so it was not likely I would be talking anyone into changing their minds. We all agreed we would make it work and I am forever grateful for their love and hospitality.

We happened to have one young lady living in our trailer on our property and another staying in our guest room in our house in California when all of this took place. Another very dear friend familiar with things at our place was available and a great help as well. So, with just some occasional direction from us, our home was being taken care of quite well during this time. A fire, a wind event, and a power outage in our community while we were away each presented a challenge of sorts, but the ladies, whom we consider to be family, stepped up and took care of business.

Our home church family, Wes' Toms River church family, and a former Pastor of ours and his church family in Missouri of all places were a constant strength to us the entire time. We received cards, flowers, Facebook encouragements, prayers, and texts on a daily basis. I have heard it said that love heals all wounds and there is no better love than the love of family. We had family loving on us every way we turned. Of course, Wes and his family and their hospitality and love. My children that could make it there and those who could not overwhelmed me with their love. All of my grandchildren were a constant strength. My siblings shared their love and concern daily. Even my Forest Service family and SDG&E family from my previous careers made certain they were included in updates and offered their help in wonderful ways. One dear friend offered to drive his motor home from San Diego to New Jersey to drive us home to avoid flying. In His Steps, a ministry that Dolores and I are both board members and teachers, came together to pray for us daily and even took a love offering to help us financially as they knew there would be unexpected costs involved. In His Steps is family to us.

Family played a critical role in my recovery. Sadly, we sometimes take family for granted, it's easy to do. We sometimes hurt each other and/or inadvertently sever relationships with family members. Sometimes intentionally, sometimes not. We often forget to value appropriately what it means to have family, what it means to be there for each other. All of this is at our own expense since a loving family can be such an incredible strength. I shared in another chapter of the many broken relationships within my family while growing up and beyond. My dad with his dad; my brother with our dad; he with his children and his siblings. It is heartbreaking to see the pain this produces and to know the happiness that too often was missed out on. Unconditional love is the key. I have discovered that unconditional love is not always easy, but well worth the battle and fight to obtain. It is critical to the strength of all of our relationships. The more we embrace it, both inwardly and outwardly, the easier solid loving relationships become to have and to protect. We are by nature imperfect beings. So, it is not easy to always act in an appropriate or loving way. I have found the more I acknowledge this fact, the more grace I can have for others and their difficulty or struggle with this very same issue. We all fall short! We can learn to love and appreciate that about each other and as a result begin to whittle away all of the "conditions" we put on love.

My family, all of them stepped up for me when I needed them most. My wife, my children, grandchildren, friends, co-workers, church members, and more were all there when I needed them most. I could not appreciate them more.

I am proud to say that there is nothing my family could do to ever make me stop loving them. There is nothing they could do to ever cause me to stop speaking to them. There is nothing they could do to make me think I no longer need them. And as they were for me, I will do my very best to be there for them today, tomorrow, and forever! Thank you my precious family, all of you. I love you very much!

***

Commitment is the key character trait for this chapter. My tragedy became instead a complete blessing because of the "commitment" of so many loved ones. Although I did not enjoy in any way the physical side of my heart incident, I could not appreciate more the commitment displayed by those who helped me and those I know and love. Every emergency related staff member was thoroughly committed to their profession and to saving lives. My family and friends demonstrated unmatched commitment to my care and recovery during and following this event. Thank you Jesus for so many good people in my life!

Let Freedom Ring
(Gratitude)

CHAPTER 8

(The little boy correcting his teacher says innocently, I'm not free...I am four!)

I am not exactly what you would call a "Patriot", but I certainly love my country! I at times am embarrassed that I did not serve my country in the military. My time for that was as the Vietnam War was ending. During the years immediately preceding my eighteenth birthday men were being drafted into the Army at alarming rates. The "lottery" system was somewhat new and if young men were hesitant in anyway about joining up on their own, they played the game of "DRAFT" roulette, which could inadvertently put you in the Army. I had a definite lean towards the Air Force for my service if it became necessary. My older brother served honorably and in fact made a life career between the Air Force and the Air National Guard. I gathered the necessary information to quickly join up if necessary if my birthdate was chosen as a likely candidate to be drafted into the Army. The year before my entry into the lottery was the first to <u>not</u> select draftees from dates drawn across the entire calendar year. My Draft year was expected to be even less so...and it was. My number turned out to be unreachable, unless something changed drastically allowing me to consider other options for my immediate future. As covered in previous chapters I opted to join the U.S. Forest Service and not any of the military branches. Although not an armed service, I did always feel I was still in service to my country with my work in wildland firefighting. I have never thought it unreasonable that we all have a responsibility to work together to support and protect this incredible gift of FREEDOM God blessed us with in this country.

If you google the word freedom you find an interesting array of definitions and descriptions. It speaks to freedom as the power or right to act, speak, or think as one wants without hindrance. It discusses freedom as the absence of subjection to foreign domination or authoritarian government. And it also alludes to freedom as a state free from prison and not enslaved. And I am sure there are an infinite number of additional similar thoughts on the term freedom. But here are some of mine developed through both research and a lot of life experience.

First off let's look at what "Freedom" is. For us in America, freedom is this tall lady who stands in the middle of the New York harbor holding high a torch that cries out to all of America...we are free! Freedom is definitely Biblical and a gift from God for those of us who believe. Multiple Old and New Testament stories discuss freedom. In Galatians 5:13-14 it states "You, my brothers and sisters, were called to be free. But do not use your freedom to indulge the flesh; rather, serve one another humbly in love. For the entire law is fulfilled in keeping this one command: "Love your neighbor as yourself". John 8: 36 "So if the Son sets you free, you will be free indeed".

And in 2 Corinthians 3: 17 "Now the Lord is the Spirit, and where the Spirit of the Lord is, there is freedom".

Freedom is a God given gift available to all at no physical cost. But as result of our freedom we are asked to serve one another in love. This important caveat is the key to our individual freedoms not conflicting with or compromising the freedom of others.

Here are a few things that "Freedom" is not. It <u>is not</u> the right to do anything regardless of the consequences. It <u>is not</u> the right to practice or indulge in your freedom at the expense of others. It <u>is not</u> an excuse for falling short. It <u>is not</u> empowerment, entitlement, or a list of personal rights. Freedom <u>is not</u> entirely free as it comes with enormous responsibility. For the concept of freedom to work we must approach it with extreme humility, care and concern for others.

Nelson Mandela once said, "For to be free is not merely to cast off one's chains, but to live in a way that respects and enhances the freedom of others."

In the Old Testament book of Exodus, the theme of freedom for the Jewish people is the heart of the story. In God's covenant with Abraham he predicted the bondage and suffering of the Hebrews. The hope for deliverance of the Israelites through Moses spoke of freedom in a profound sense. The purpose of this freedom was for the people to be able to serve God and obey His laws. We so often think of freedom as the right to do as we please, when in fact it should be thought of as the right to love, honor, and obey the living Lord. Throughout the Old Testament the Israelites struggled continuously to obey God's commands usually resulting in destruction or them ending up in captivity. As individuals and as a people, they just could not live as their law commanded them to. That is where Jesus enters the story. He came as the ultimate sacrifice for all their discretions and to be an example for all to follow. He came with the promise of freedom for all. He came with messages opposing the proud and exalting the humble and the oppressed. He represented a freedom completely unheard of before.

The theme of freedom resonates throughout the Bible with perhaps two strikingly familiar verses, one from the Old Testament book of Isaiah and one from the New Testament book of Luke saying it best. Both essentially sharing that the Spirit of the Lord is on us. We are appointed to proclaim the good news to the poor, proclaim freedom for prisoners, recovery of sight for the blind, and to set the oppressed free. It is our duty to promote and protect our freedom.

Now as we leap forward some 1700 plus years we find another "Freedom" story as recorded in history.

The 4th of July, Independence Day is the national holiday of the United States of America commemorating the signing of the Declaration of Independence by the Continental Congress on July 4, 1776, in Philadelphia, Pennsylvania.

At the time of the signing the US consisted of 13 colonies under the rule of England's King George III. There was growing unrest in the colonies concerning the taxes that had to be paid to England. This was commonly referred to as "Taxation without Representation" as the colonists did not have any representation in the English Parliament and had no say in what went on. As the unrest grew in the colonies, King George sent extra troops to help control any rebellion.

In 1774 the 13 colonies sent delegates to Philadelphia Pennsylvania to form the First Continental Congress. The delegates were unhappy with England but were not yet ready to declare war.

In April 1775 as the King's troops advanced on Concord Massachusetts Paul Revere would sound the alarm that "The British are coming; the British are coming" as he rode his horse through the late-night streets.

The battle of Concord and its "shot heard round the world" would mark the unofficial beginning of the colonies' war for Independence.

The following May the colonies again sent delegates to the Second Continental Congress. For almost a year the congress tried to work out its differences with England, again without formally declaring war.

By June 1776 their efforts had become hopeless and a committee was formed to compose a formal declaration of independence. Headed by Thomas Jefferson, the committee included John Adams, Benjamin Franklin, Robert R. Livingston and Roger Sherman. Thomas Jefferson was chosen to write the first draft which was presented to the Congress on June 28. After various changes a vote was taken late in the afternoon of July 4th. Of the 13 colonies, 9 voted in favor of the Declaration, 2 – Pennsylvania and South Carolina voted No, Delaware undecided and New York abstained. To make it official John Hancock, President of the Continental Congress, signed the Declaration of Independence. It is said that John Hancock signed his name "with a great flourish" so "King George could read it without his spectacles!"

The following day copies of the Declaration were distributed. The first newspaper to print the Declaration was the Pennsylvania Evening Post on July 6, 1776. On July 8th the Declaration had its first public reading in Philadelphia's Independence Square. Twice that day the Declaration was read to cheering crowds and ringing church bells. Even the bell in Independence Hall was rung. The "Province Bell" would later be renamed the "Liberty Bell".

And although the signing of the Declaration was not completed until August, the 4th of July has been accepted as the official anniversary of United States independence. The first Independence Day celebration took place the following year – July 4, 1777. By the early 1800s the traditions of parades, picnics, and fireworks were established as the way to celebrate America's birthday and more importantly "American Freedom". And although fireworks have been banned in many places, most towns and cities usually have big firework displays for all to see and enjoy annually on this most treasured day.

America did not seek Freedom and obtain it so that we as a country could then do whatever the heck we please. We sought freedom for the very same reasons our forefathers before us did…so we could serve God and obey His laws without influence from outside governance or not. This was so that we too could have a country free from oppression…that strives to bring down the proud and exalt the humble. So that we could live in a place where all men, and of course all women are created equal; and that we would be endowed by our Creator with certain inalienable rights; among which are Life, Liberty, and the Pursuit of Happiness. This place is the United States of America.

We, I included, sometimes take our freedom for granted. Here in the United States we are a nation based on the concept of freedom. We sometimes abuse it's intent, but always in our core is the knowledge and understanding that we are a free people. When we dishonor this privilege, we have laws and a constitution that protect our rights even if it isn't always instant or automatic. It takes only a cursory glance at other destitute parts of our globe to see where God's people are grossly oppressed and exploited and seriously lack freedom. We fail at times to appreciate our good fortune here in America.

Slavery is weaved in and out throughout history affecting the lives of so many. It is in early Biblical times worldwide and in America during its early history up and just beyond the Civil War. This perhaps causing the greatest controversy in our country since its founding. Slavery is the antithesis of freedom and laughs in the face of God's desire for us to love Him and our neighbor as ourselves.

The way our country obtained and maintains our freedom is through a united responsibility as individuals coming together as one, for the good of us all. We need to take that responsibility seriously if we want to protect forever what we have. Certainly, all things are not perfect in our country, but we should not focus on the imperfections and instead celebrate our many blessings. We should not get so caught up in "they" have taken God out of our schools, "they" have compromised the Constitution of the United States, "they" no longer truly support equality, because folks we are the "they". We can make and keep this country great if we choose to do so…or we can do as the Israelites before us did, forgetting

God's liberating work, giving over to destruction and captivity. I suggest instead that we honor our freedom and demonstrate it by serving God, obeying His laws, and loving our neighbor as ourselves. It is entirely up to the collective us, God Bless America, thank you!

***

I selected gratitude as the character trait for freedom as I can think of almost nothing more deserving of our gratitude than our freedom. Thankfulness and appreciation are keys to our will and desire to protect and cherish what we have. I am so grateful for my freedom and for the freedom of others!

Counting My Steps
Health

CHAPTER 9

(If we shouldn't eat at night, why did they put a light in refrigerators?)

Almost 8 years ago my oldest daughter Wendy (I don't dare share her age) and I hiked up Mt. Whitney with some dear friends from our hometown of Ramona. This mountain famous for being the highest peak in the continental United States rises to a height of 14,505' or so, depending on your source of information. From the trailhead beginning at Whitney Portal, elevation 8,360', you ascend approximately 6100' to summit at the peak after about 11 miles leading to an eventual 22-mile round trip. We did an up and back in one day taking about 16 hours to complete the round trip.

We were both running regularly at the time and felt half marathon type mileages was enough training leading up to this hike. WRONG! Not so at all. Not only were we short in the training department, but not doing the right training for the task. So, as my wife vividly recalls as she took us to our hotel room post hike, the two of us proclaimed we would never do that again in our life. We were beat up, sore, fatigued beyond description and absolutely done with Mt. Whitney and its "highest peak in the United States stuff".

So as the saying goes, "never say never"! A little over a year ago, my 16-year-old Grandson Jackson (Wendy's son) expressed interest in hiking Mt. Whitney. Not an overly ambitious desire for an active young teenager but let me tell you about Jackson. Jackson has had seven heart surgeries three of which were open-heart in his not so lengthy life to date. The most recent was open-heart and just months before this request to do Whitney. He is a miraculous survivor who let's nothing hold him back. So, with Cardiologist approval and mom's as well, the seed was planted for our journey. Papa and mom were on the hook for another Mt. Whitney adventure!

With Jackson as our inspiration the potential participants grew in the following months. His mom, dad, and younger brother (with strong parental encouragement) threw their hat in. My son Joel, his wife Becky, her sister Michelle, my Great Nephew Alex and friends Tiffany, Kristi, Bob Denny, and Jason Winters came on board. My special hiking partner Rebecca was in too. Fourteen hikers altogether. There was no guarantee we could procure permits for a group this large on the date or alternate date we desired. Our persistence paid off as we got all the permits we needed after multiple efforts. I was just excited at the interest by so many. We came from all over the San Diego area and Wendy's family from a town in central California near Yosemite National Park. Bob, Jason, Alex, Rebecca and I all called Ramona, CA home.

Rebecca and I worked hard locally to prepare. The hub of our fitness training was on Mt. Woodson here in Ramona. Mt. Woodson is a terrific workout with its unrelenting steepness even though somewhat short lived at 2 miles up to the summit. Already regulars on the mountain we increased our frequency, distance, and speed progressively through the months preceding our hike. Occasionally we would extend the hike from Ramona to the top of Woodson, down to Poway Lake and back for a total of 11 miles. We also added other hikes adjacent to or near Ramona, many of which are the most difficult within the area. We concluded our training one week before by hiking Mt. Baldy in Rancho Cucamonga. This approximate 12-mile round trip involved 4,000' elevation gain and served as a great precursor to our big event. This time I felt like I was training for the task at hand and should end up better prepared. For me, then 66 years young, training would be critical.

We got our first choice of dates and the hike was scheduled as an up and back on Monday August 6, 2018 for the whole group. We traveled up the preceding Saturday, did an acclimation hike on Sunday and prepared to take-off from Whitney Portal at zero dark thirty or precisely 3:00 a.m. early Monday pre-dawn. Our group was a motley sort comprised mostly of family and an assorted few who could stand being with us for that long. Our core group of 12 ranged in age from 15 – 66 with 6 males and 6 females. Two others, Bob and Jason, started with us but planned from the beginning to complete just what Bob was up for with some serious arthritis issues cropping up just prior to our hike. All had prepared in a variety of ways and only Wendy, Bob, Tiffany, and I had the pleasure of experiencing Mt. Whitney previously.

The hike went very well overall. Some of the group much faster than the others but all were steady for the most part working our way up slowly to the top. As part of the permit process each hiker is issued a wag bag or more affectionately known as a "poop" bag and yes you are required to carry out waste products created by your body. At the beginning of the hike very little was shared or discussed about this somewhat embarrassing topic, but by the end even the ladies were boasting about how many times they had successfully used their bag. This, pee breaks, and female time of the month issues made for interesting trail talk and I, even with a wife and two daughters never learned more in a 24-hour period about "feminine hygiene"!

The team worked well together and the last small group of us summited the peak by 1:30 that afternoon, on schedule for our hopefully 16 hr. round trip. We high fived, congratulated each other, caught up on some hydration and calories, and took a bundle of pictures to document our stunning feat before heading down. Down is not as easy as one might think. There is a lot of torque on the joints and of course you have put many tough miles on your body already. For the most part the return trip was going very well until our Kristi slipped right in front of me and snapped her ankle pretty good. I guess chivalry may be dead as I did not cast myself swiftly beneath her to cushion the fall but instead she ended up on the ground with a severely sprained ankle. All kidding aside it was a pretty serious injury and Kristi, Rebecca, and I were slightly separated from the others. Hikers passing by helped get the word to our larger group. Well, both my son Joel and I are trained to some degree as 1st Responders from our job as firefighters. I had an ace bandage to immobilize the ankle the best I could, and we made crutches out of hiking poles, sophisticated ones at that. We were about 6 miles from the bottom when it happened. We knew it would take some time, so we did our best to get Kristi down the hill safely. We met up with some of the others and everyone did what they could to make her journey less miserable. Alex, completely exhausted at the bottom, came back up the mountain to help us after getting the word about the incident. Several hours post incident we sent all the ladies the rest of way down the hill and Joel, Alex, and I continued to help Kristi the remainder of the way. What a trooper she was; no complaints, pushed through the pain, remained lighthearted, and showed keen appreciation for what was going on. At about 1:30 in the morning we reached the trailhead and returned to our lodging sites with an extended adventure that now totaled 24 very long hours.

Despite our incident it was still an incredibly successful event. Those planning to summit did. Those who did not plan to make it, made it further than they planned. And with one small exception, everybody made it back safely and all now with a pretty good story to tell.

Will we ever do Mt. Whitney again? I don't know as I truly did learn, *"never say never!"*

So, what does this have to do with "counting my steps"? Counting steps is a fairly contemporary means to encourage folks to increase their physical activity. Whether it be a "FitBit" or one of an assortment of phone apps made just for this purpose; it has successfully boosted the general population's focus on physical fitness. These devices miraculously record your daily physical activity, providing you remember to have them with you throughout the day. "How many steps do you have?" is now as customary a greeting between people as once was "Hello, how have you been?". Or, "I can't join you just now as I have to get the rest of my steps!" is a response to all too many invitations for folks to spend time together. Many late-night quick little jaunts in total darkness have been taken in haste (and mildly dangerous) just to lock in those last few "steps" to make a daily goal. So, sarcasm aside, is this a good thing or just another annoying fad destined to fall by the wayside sooner than later? I believe it to be an incredible motivator that encourages people to genuinely maintain and even improve their commitment to physical fitness.

To my good fortune "Physical Fitness" has always been somewhat of a priority in my life. For a starter I was always actively involved in sports both sandlot and organized, that at least minimally encouraged some physical activity. This was as a pre-teen, through high school, and continued into adulthood. In Junior High and High School, I was on the wrestling team and also did one brief year in High School gymnastics. I was an above average wrestler and a definite "work in progress" in the gymnastics' arena. Although not especially proficient in the assorted events of this sport, the physical conditioning in gymnastics was irreplaceable. The blessing or take-away from all of this was a solid foundation for the role physical fitness would play going forward in my life. I loved working out! I loved being in shape. At this point in my life however I really had no place for running or arduous hiking. Muscle tone and six-packs were the primary motivators.

After high school I went directly into firefighting on a "Hotshot" crew in the U.S. Forest Service. The conditioning required for this made anything I had done prior seem sophomoric, definitely inadequate for such a physically demanding job such as this. In preparation for fire season we had a "boot camp" style first two weeks with 8 grueling hours of physical training and arduous work daily. I had never worked out much over 2 hours in a day for any of my previous fitness endeavors. We started with calisthenics to warm up; followed by an excruciating number of sit-ups push-ups, pull-ups, and bar dips. Next we would do a 3-5-mile run (completely new to me) or an even farther hike with full gear on in the 90-100-degree heat of Southern California. And then we would pretty much spend the rest of the day cutting practice fire line, again in the warmth of the early summer blistering heat. And speaking of blisters…I had blister on my blisters adding a little bodily pain element to the already mind-blowing new life experience. Little did I know that this was just a glimpse of the physical requirements necessary to actually perform the duties involved in the actual suppression of a fast-moving wildfire. That is another story in itself.

    Staying in shape was an ever-growing staple in my life. As I promoted in the Forest Service and my job became less physical I vowed to keep up a physical maintenance program. I would do some minimal daily work out and try to run about 3 miles a day in spite of my lack of love for the quasi-sport called jogging. During my time as a Battalion Chief I got a new boss who had the reputation as an extreme long-distance runner; marathons, ultra-marathons and even 100-mile races through the desert. In one of our first discussions he suggested we start running together every opportunity we could. I let him know that I run 3 miles and only 3 miles; not even 3.1. I insisted that this was perfectly clear to him so there would be no expectation of me joining in his insanity. Well so much for perfectly clear. Over the next several months he incrementally increased our distance such that I was okay with just a little more a bit at a time. He also increased the hills and steepness involved. To cut to the chase he had me enrolled and then participate in an ultra-marathon within about 6 months of his arrival. This run was 26.2 miles with an elevation gain of over 2500'…please note, I never claimed to be the brightest lamp in the room!

Basically, from that point on I was a jogger of sorts. During my time in the tree business I ran much less but worked nearly as hard daily as in my previous firefighting days. I continued to jog frequently though, as I am really an "addict" by nature. I was never fast or especially good but definitely consistent. I used to say I run mile 1 in 10 minutes, and I run mile 26 in 10 minutes. Over the years I got my miles down into the mid-9's and always excited anytime they were under 10. I would tease my rather swift sons that they might run faster than me, but if we raced I could just keep going until I won. Over the years until my mid-fifties I ran in 4 marathons and 10 or so half marathons. The actual events paled in comparison to the training required to be able to complete one. Needless to say, I stayed in relatively good shape. The last dozen years or so I have focused more on hiking, mostly steep terrain hiking including some pretty cool adventures. This lifetime commitment to physical fitness may have saved my life in my recent Aortic Dissection open-heart surgery according to the doctors and other medical staff. For that I am grateful!

In multiple spots throughout my sharing I have alluded to my propensity towards addictions both good and bad. When I was struggling with drugs and alcohol, I did so with a zealousness that easily could have led to my incarceration or even to the cause of my death. I was all in, to a fault and for that I have much regret. But the same addictive nature has been a blessing to me when it comes to taking care of myself physically. I work out with the same zeal and vigor I put into other aspects of my life and for that I am grateful.

So about 2 years ago my wife put an "app" on my phone for me to try out. It records my steps, my mileage, and calories burned on both a daily and monthly basis. I never needed anything like that before so why would I now was my basic attitude upon receipt. Let me tell you, I now "count my steps" every day. I have daily goals and I have monthly goals. You wouldn't believe how many silly things I have done to make sure I reach my daily goal or to give my month the proper number of total steps. Remember that "addictive nature" thing? I am addicted to counting my steps! And nowadays I find myself engaging people when I see them with a question, "how many steps do you have today?" I guess that's not so bad!

***

Health is my chosen character attribute for "Counting My Steps". I imagine a case could be made that "health" is not particularly a character attribute but a physical state of our being. It's okay you can correct that in your book when you write it. For me it is a part of my inner being, my character. I think, in general, good health makes us mentally more solid and complete as a person. It goes beyond physical fitness and includes just caring for our body and all of its organs. Caring for our health can make us stronger inside and out. This helps us to improve on all of our other character attributes involved in our life process.

Go Slow To Go Fast
Patience

CHAPTER 10

(My three favorite things are eating my family and not using commas!)

I have been the lead builder for the construction of about 60 homes in Mexico with an organization called Corazon. These homes are constructed in one day with our motto being "Helping to change the life of a family forever in just one day!" As a Construction Superintendent, I am a pretty good fireman. In other words, my expertise in life does not lie in the construction arena as I have very limited experience. Fortunately, the house we build is a very simple 16' × 20' wood construction with interior loft and asphalt shingle roof. I participated as a worker in a number of builds before I was "ordained" as a "Lead Builder". My promotion had much more to do with my willingness to do this than my ability as a builder. Willing volunteers can be a valuable commodity to any charitable endeavor. Most of the builds I have participated in and supervised were done by my home church, which to my good fortune, happens to have many skilled participants. Many are much more skilled than I. A few times I was placed with a group or groups that had limited skill and that always made for a much more interesting experience for me and for them. But by the grace of God we somehow succeeded each time. Regardless, over time I became familiar with all aspects of the build and was able to supervise it with a reduced anxiety factor as well as increased proficiency. Although not extremely complex, the house does take some organization, prioritizing, timing, and oversight for the day's build to go reasonably well. In addition to skilled help, there is always novice participants anxious to help in any way they can. We have a "Corazon" way to construct these homes that purposely allows for all to participate and feel a part of this life changing experience. Sometimes that frustrates the skilled labor but after sometimes multiple caring explanations, most of the professionals understand the value of doing it this way. Generally, I kick off each build with a bit of a tease. "If you see or know of a better way to accomplish any of our tasks today, please feel free to share with me…immediately upon completion of today's project. Today however we will do it the Corazon way." In reality we will always do it the Corazon way. It purposefully blesses more people. I have observed much biting of the tongue by our skilled professionals as we at times archaically proceed in a somewhat amateurish manner. No nail guns, no paint sprayers, just lots of helpers with hammers, nails, and paint brushes. Not as efficient but it intentionally engages many more folks.

The beauty of these builds is that the pros and novices alike are there for the same purpose, to help their neighbor and share the love! So, this being said it is my job to make sure everyone gets the opportunity to do so. What I try to do is break up the project into smaller components such as roof, walls, painting, loft, stairs etc. and identify a leader for each.

My leaders know we are more interested in full participation by all, as opposed to knocking it out quickly in a professionally efficient manner. This sounds great on paper but is not always the case. At times overly ambitious first timers hit the ground running at breakneck speed with little to no understanding of the big picture. Often their well-intended efforts can inadvertently sabotage the overall process. They will jump in and start cutting, nailing, or painting indiscriminately without guidance or direction. So, rule #1 for all is GO SLOW TO GO FAST!

In the case of these home builds as well as life in general, going slow and methodically can actually expedite the completion of our project or in any life endeavor as well. It truly works at Corazon. Painters who have hastily painted the wrong side of the siding without direction have slowed the process considerably. Overly helpful nailers prematurely nailing siding on a wall where a window needs to go results in tearing it off and starting over. The list goes on where an urgent desire to "do" inadvertently complicates the overall project considerably and delays its completion.

Life can certainly be that way too. For some reason we have propensity to rush into things, take short cuts, or dead head to our target without adequate considerations. Somewhere in my vast collection of wisdoms I picked up an acronym that really stuck with me. Please forgive my mild crassness. The seven P's…*proper prior planning prevents piss poor performance*. Needless to say, this stuck with me and I think of it often. We sometimes skirt around proper prior planning in an effort to save time when in reality it almost always costs us both time and efficiency.

A big part of the end of my career in the U.S. Forest Service was serving as a National Type 1 Incident Commander *(discussed briefly in an earlier chapter)* on a National Incident Management Team. We were one of 16 teams comprised of about 50 emergency management experts who would be brought in to manage the most complex incidents in the country and at times outside of the country. Although primarily we dealt with large wildfires; we also were involved with the Northridge Earthquake, the Columbia Shuttle Recovery, and multiple hurricanes on the eastern seaboard and in the Caribbean Islands. Ordination as a Type 1 Incident Commander was not simply because I was willing to do the job as it was for Lead Builder with Corazon. I had decades of experience working at every level between firefighter recruit all the way to I.C. I had position specific training at every level with extensive competency tests and verifications at each level before advancement as well. An I.C. friend of mine in Montana once calculated that by the time we reached the Incident Commander level we had an equivalent amount of classroom and field work to that of a Medical Doctor. My point being we were well prepared for our duties by following and adhering to strict guidelines and requirements within the Incident Command System. ICS is a tried and true means to manage complex incidents. Without great detail I will state it goes way beyond the de-escalation of a critical emergency. ICS teaches and preaches a comprehensive planning process which precedes any tactical operations necessary to mitigate an incident. It incorporates logistical planning and support required to adequately provide for the incident and care for the incident participants. It even manages the financial aspects, medical, human resources, and more. So why the sudden education on Emergency Management?

Any true emergency generates an immediate sense of urgency. Management of said emergency requires the need for expeditious handling of the situation. The priorities for us were always these and in this order: life, property, and then the environment. Each of these priorities cries for imminent action, but FAST is not always the best. I have the good fortune (or simply being old enough) to have fought fire during both the pre-ICS and post-ICS periods. Pre-ICS was about FAST and furious. Get a lot of stuff on it as quickly as possible. Now that still works for what we call "Initial Attack" or the first actions taken while a fire is relatively small and somewhat manageable. It is not so good when it is not. Pre-ICS we Initial Attack(ed) a fire at its beginning and then basically over and over again even if it was off and running, usually to no avail. Post-ICS we now use initial attack tactics in the beginning while simultaneously going into long-range planning and more comprehensive management of the incident. We go slow to go FAST! Although not perfect it has proved remarkably more effective.

Going slow to go fast is not just about tactical activities in our life such as home construction and firefighting. This mantra can also work in our basic decision-making processes on a daily basis. It can and should be used in helping with the setting of our life priorities. It can play an appreciable role in both our short-term and long-term planning for most anything we do. Again, proper prior planning prevents piss poor performance I heard somewhere before. A tenet to live by! Planning is an incredible tool we too often forget to use. It can be such a key to success. In ICS (Incident Command System), there is an entire function of the Command Staff dedicated to nothing but planning for the mitigation of a major emergency. It intentionally forces us to methodically discern the best path to take for the operation we are preparing for. If I may stay in ICS for just a bit, I think the planning organization and duties related to each within ICS will reinforce "planning's" value for integrating it into more of our life decisions and future direction. The Planning Section was led and directed by the Planning Section Chief, who reported directly to the Incident Commander. He/She had the overall responsibility to ensure the Operational tactics (i.e. firefighting and other emergency related work) was based on a good well thought out plan with as many kinks or potential obstacles removed or mitigated ahead of time. Again, proper prior planning! The sub-staff to the PSC included a Situation Unit Leader, Resource Unit Leader, Documentation Unit Leader, and Demobilization Unit Leader. Please bear with me I promise to not go too deep in spite of my love for this incredible tool. The Situation leader was responsible for obtaining and displaying all pertinent information related to the incident; be it maps, situational updates, hazards related to the incident, and more. The Resource leader would track every resource involved with the incident and their personnel. They would know who was assigned, who is resting, and who is available for immediate response. The Documentation leader was responsible for documentation to memorialize the incident activity for historical, legal, and other potential post-incident needs. Demobilization leaders specifically planned for the downsizing of the incident and travel arrangements home for the resources that required such. To the outsider this may seem like overkill, but to the emergency manager it infinitely improved how we conducted business. So, if we use the principles in our planning and not necessarily the whole Incident Command System process...I think a case could be made for improvement in how we conduct our life. Before blindly jumping into some of our more complex decisions we instead take the time to plan appropriately. We assess the situation first. What exactly is involved, and do we have all the facts? Do we have good situational awareness? Is there a history or previous experience we can incorporate into our decision? What resources do we need to pull this off? Are they available? How do we procure them if not? Let's document this. Do we need a list, or would a written plan make things go much better? The more energy we put into the planning the better our decisions and/or actions will be. Remember to go slow to go fast. Have I mentioned that before.

***

Patience is the character attribute for this chapter of "Go Slow to Go Fast". Patience is a virtue, so they say. And for good reason! Being virtuous is no easy task just as being patient is extremely difficult in and of itself. I don't know about you, but I struggle big time with patience. I pray for patience constantly and then get upset that it doesn't happen quick enough. My goal then is to progressively improve my patience going forward and to be okay with the fact that it is a slow process. How about you?

With God Good, Without God Bad

Faith

CHAPTER 11

(As long as there are tests, there will be prayer in school)

There is a part of me that thinks "With God Good, Without God Bad!" no duh...end of chapter. But sadly for you, I am going to expound on that a bit, and you will have more to read. I realize that both potential readers of this book (or hopefully I mean all potential readers of this book) might not share the same opinion of God as a creator, heavenly Father, and life guide. In fact, there are likely dozens or more combinations of thoughts and beliefs among our readers just like in life itself. What I share however will be factual and the truth...for me! You then would be welcome to believe and use any part or all of it to support or modify your truth! Or of course opt to leave your beliefs unchanged.

Briefly in Chapter 1, I shared a little bit about my faith walk and periodically throughout the book I touched briefly on it here and there. I would like to now go into it in more detail. Not to put my beliefs on to you necessarily but instead to share what has been good for me and what has not. What you do with it is entirely up to you.

If my memory and tales of my life serve me correctly, I started attending church around Kindergarten or just before. Actually, this would have been Sunday School for the most part and "big" church as we called it during major holidays mostly. My mom was the one engaged in church as dad did not participate at all. He was raised a Catholic, more or less forced to participate, and basically grew up and out of the desire to attend church. Mom went to church intermittently throughout her childhood and apparently found value in attending. We attended what I now know to be a somewhat progressive church, certainly "left" of the much more conservative churches of the time. It was very traditional for the most part. Mom taught Sunday School and made sure we were there basically every week. Although we didn't study the Bible in any depth, we did learn many of the traditional Bible Stories. I definitely received the foundational belief that God is good!

We attended church through the bulk of my adolescent years. I developed what I call an "outward" relationship with God and I guess I thought that the Jesus thing was a pretty cool happening. You know…baby, in a manger, Christmas et al. I suppose I believed God was the creator of the Universe, but He was a distant almost inanimate being that if anything I feared more than truly loved. All that being said, I did think of Him as a promoter of "good" and defender against "evil". There was nothing intimate at that time in our relationship. I went to church first because I basically was required to. I enjoyed the community and the good nature of the teachings. As I got into Junior High I loved Youth Group. This was more for the social aspect, including a girlfriend or two, than the Christian content or teachings. Nonetheless, I attended regularly and count it an overall positive time in my life. As I grew smarter, relative to when I was less smart, I recognized that my life definitely had its share of dysfunction.

My High School days brought about a drifting away from church for the most part. I don't recall why mom no longer took us or required us to go, I just know we stopped. I admittedly continued until the girlfriends stopped and then had no further need for church or Youth Group at that time in my life.

My next religious encounter, for a lack of a better term, happened as my High School days were ending and my girlfriend, soon to be fiancé, and eventually my first wife attended church on a regular basis. It was an extremely conservative church and her Uncle was the Pastor. They went to church more than just Sunday. There was Bible Studies, Choirs, Church Services, Meetings, Service projects, and more. My Father-in-law Gordie was actively involved. These people were at church all the "freaking" time! This was certainly something new to me. Her Uncle Ed, the Pastor, looking back literally scared me to death. When we got engaged he required us to attend pre-marital counseling, with him! Spooky, I even had a dream he was riding a black horse, dressed in all black, with a black cape and hat waving a sword as he rode by me commanding me to get to church! All kidding aside, I was probably becoming less drawn to church than more. I did what I needed to make things work for us for the most part. Interestingly as time went on I realized my new Father-in-law was perhaps the nicest person I had ever met. One hundred percent legit, no pretense. He was the epitome of "good". Still not investigating personally to a deeper level about this faith stuff, I was smart enough to recognize his kindness was God related at least in his mind. His strong belief taught him to love others in a big way. Sadly, that marriage ended up in divorce and Gordon has since passed, but I loved him to the end and forever will appreciate what he shared with me.

My life hit lots of bumps pre & post-divorce from my first wife that have already been detailed to a fault. So, let's jump ahead to my literal "Come to Jesus" life changing event, also detailed in an earlier chapter. Without re-iterating every last detail let's revisit my final fall and that life changing Jesus moment that lifted me up. So, at the depths of my spiral down, addicted to both drugs and alcohol, and living on property we had been evicted from, my wife (to be) and I were in a horrid fight. We were in a camper shell and our daughter was trying to sleep in the overhead while we yelled and screamed at each other. Mid-argument I looked at my daughter and had a revelation that this is not where I was supposed to end up. Without detailing the rest, I was able to become completely drug/alcohol free, return to the Forest Service, and join a church hoping to get some extra "good" in my life.

My life began instantly to have more easily discernable good in it. We married and moved to Ramona. We joined a church (the one I am still a member of 31 years later) and I became incredibly involved. Things did not work out for my wife and I as she preferred much of the old lifestyle. I bet I was not particularly easy to live with while motoring though my new life journey at full speed. We ended up divorced. I was fully engaged in my newfound or perhaps you might say renewed faith. I went to church, Bible Study, Men's group, mission projects, church socials, and pretty much anything church related I could dig my hands into. This time I learned about a different God, a different Jesus. Not because others had taught me wrong but instead I finally opened my eyes to the truth. I could have a personal and even intimate relationship with Jesus and that was good. I know now that it was Jesus who spoke to me in the midst of that horrid fight. He knew I wanted more, I wanted different, and He helped me to make it happen.

I did not instantly become this perfect person and in fact am still very far from perfect. My goal each day is to do better and move even just a little in that perfect direction. That perfect direction for me is the triune God: The Father, Son, and Holy Spirit.

Miraculous things have happened since that time. I met and married my wife Dolores who is the love of my life. We enjoy and love church together. We love our kids, extended family, friends, and others to the best of our ability and as He teaches us to do. We do our best to serve Him whenever called to do so. Life is good!

Let me summarize this story as it relates to "With God Good, Without God Bad". My childhood, again not without some love and caring, had a lot of chaos mixed in throughout. There was drinking and arguing and discontent routinely. Without God some of those times were bad. The good during those times was when love won out. Love that was invented by God, by Jesus Christ. Our church experience at that time, though not award winning by any stretch, still instilled a foundation in me. That foundation with God was good.

During my first marriage the love my Father-in-law radiated was good. My lack of joining in was bad. My drug and alcohol abuse period in my life without God was definitely bad. My come to Jesus moment and going forward moment from there, certainly good.

It is not Rocket Science that receiving help to be a better person is a good thing. There are probably other alternative means to achieve goodness and I would not dispute or try to oversell my means as the only way. See, I believe in my heart that good is of God and all good…is good! Say that three times fast. My life is a testimony to this, and I am blessed to have the opportunity to share with anyone and everyone who would like to at least give it a try.

***

Faith is the character attribute for this chapter. The Bible in Hebrews 11:1 states, "Now faith is the substance of things hoped for, the evidence of things not seen". Just as I have not seen the wind, but only the evidence of it, I believe in wind. I have not actually seen God create good, but truly have witnessed the evidence of it. I believe strongly GOD IS GOOD and With God good, without God bad!

Thank You & Good-Bye

CHAPTER 12

(I am not completely useless, I can at least be used as a bad example for others!)

Thank you, this has been fun for me. I hope it was at least to some degree for you as well. If you are reading this closing I am going to assume you read the bulk of the book, as who would jump to the end without reading at least some of its content?

So, I guess I wrote a book? Good, bad, or indifferent...I wrote a book! I shared a lot about me and my life to this point, but there is one thing I didn't bring up that I will now. A lifelong problem for me has been that I don't always complete things. Not necessarily small everyday tasks but more about the big things in life. I did fairly well academically in school and had every intention of going to college and completing it. I went intermittently but never came close to getting a degree. I shared about my Forest Service career, which overall was a positive experience, but my leaving it early in my career and again just short of mandatory retirement prevented me from maximum accomplishment. My role as a National Incident Commander was rewarding and yet I only did it just over 1 year and then left the Forest Service. There are other examples, but my point is if we had "do-overs" like in the comedy City

Slickers alludes to, I would do a handful or more things quite differently and for sure more completely. I imagine we can all say that to some degree, but I truly wish I had been blessed with better follow through. That being said, I wrote a book! And for that I am well pleased.

I have been contemplating this book, gathering thoughts, made notes, initiated some stories for several years now. I got more serious over the last couple of years but worked very intermittently and infrequently during this time. I never lost interest but lacked dedication to finishing it. It took a unique motivation to get me going strong and I hope my special motivator was not from God, for just me, at the expense of others. The famous Covid-19 virus, better known as the Corona Virus, locked an entire nation (or world for that matter) down for months. Life had a propensity to become somewhat boring for a while. To my good fortune (and maybe not so for yours) I chose to get in gear with this project. And it worked. Sorry you had to suffer this horrible inconvenience so I could finish my book. I thank God it's done!

I need to thank some individuals as well. First because it is the responsible thing to do and second because they truly were a blessing to my project. My wife, who put up with me and was a large part of my story, I love you and thank you! She is my friend, my lover (sorry about that tidbit), my editor, and lifetime supervisor. My daughter Wendy for her help with editing and reviewing this project for me. She was and always has been a blessing to me. And last but not least my daughter-in-law Amanda for her artwork on the book cover. I love you all!

In closing, I just want to say that there is nothing extremely special about me or my life. My experiences are similar to so many others. I just took the time to capture them in writing. It is my prayer that something I said or a thought I generated may have blessed you even a little. So, thank you (both of you) who read my book and if it is really more than two, I thank all of you very much!!!